COPING

ANXIETY

COPING WITH ANXIETY

Integrated Approaches to Treatment

Edited by
W. Walter Menninger, M.D.

JASON ARONSON INC.
Northvale, New Jersey
London

Library of Congress Cataloging-in-Publication Data

Coping with anxiety : integrated approaches to treatment / [edited by]
    W. Walter Menninger.
        p.   cm.
    Proceedings of a symposium held May 23, 1995, at the 148th Annual
Meeting of the American Psychiatric Association in Miami, Fla.
    Includes bibliographical references and index.
    ISBN: 1-56821-788-9   (sc alk. paper)
    1. Anxiety—Congresses.   2. Panic disorders—Congresses.
I. Menninger, W. Walter.   II. American Psychiatric Association.
RC531.C67   1996
616.85'223—dc20   95-51697

Manufactured in the United States of America. Jason Aronson Inc. offers books and cassettes. For information and catalog write to Jason Aronson Inc., 230 Livingston Street, Northvale, New Jersey 07647.

Contents

Acknowledgments

The material contained in *Coping with Anxiety: Integrated Approaches to Treatment* was presented on May 23, 1995, at the 148th annual meeting of the American Psychiatric Association in Miami, Florida, at an educational symposum sponsored by Menninger. The symposium was chaired by W. Walter Menninger, MD. Both the symposium and these published proceedings were supported by an unrestricted educational grant from Roche Laboratories, a member of the Roche Group.

Introduction

Marc P. DesLauriers, PhD

Anxiety disorders, the most common psychiatric illness in the United States, exhibit themselves clinically in a wide variety of ways. They range in severity from relatively mild to completely incapacitating. The vast majority of individuals suffering from these disorders are not receiving psychiatric treatment. In many cases, affected individuals seek treatment for the somatic symptoms (e.g., sweating, trembling, nausea, dizziness, heart palpitations, shortness of breath, chest pain or discomfort) but the anxiety disorder is not diagnosed. For others, the stigma or shame associated with having a "mental" or emotional illness prevents them from seeking treatment. Theories of causality have traditionally focused on either psychological stress and trauma or a biological diathesis. Current research, however, points to an interactive psychobiological model in which psychological stressors combine with biological vulnerability to precipitate and sustain the symptomatic illness.

Because of the prevalence of these conditions, researchers and clinicians continue to develop more effective treatment approaches. Although anxiety disorders themselves are not new, related conditions such as panic disorder, social phobia, and addiction present special challenges for diagnosis and treatment. The contributors to *Coping with Anxiety* present an integrated treatment approach that combines pharmacotherapy with cognitive-behavioral therapy and dynamic psychotherapy. They also identify key research issues essential for a more complete understanding of these disorders.

Jerrold Rosenbaum and his colleagues describe the phenomenology of panic disorder, as well as biological and behavioral theories of etiology. With this perspective, they review the extensive pharmacopoeia for the treatment of this condition, including selective serotonin reuptake inhibitors, tricyclic antidepressants, high-potency benzodiazepines, and certain anticonvulsants. They note that although some patients are treated effectively with these agents, most patients experience residual symptoms, continued impairment, or recurrence. In such cases, optimal outcome requires a comprehensive, integrated therapeutic program that may include a combination of drug therapy, cognitive-behavioral therapy, and psychosocial interventions.

John Marshall takes a similar approach to social phobia. After outlining prevalence and etiological factors, he highlights effective pharmacological and psychological approaches, the latter area focus-

Dr. DesLauriers is director of Continuing Education at The Menninger Clinic, Topeka, Kansas.

ing on cognitive-behavioral therapy. In light of the complexity and comorbidity associated with social phobia, he concludes that "change occurs best in the context of a therapeutic relationship in which there is trust and a subsequent feeling of safety" (p. 33).

Neither Rosenbaum and his colleagues nor Marshall espouses a particular treatment approach. Instead, they believe that clinicians need to recognize the variable expression of the disorders and select intervention strategies most suitable to the individual patient.

Kathryn Zerbe examines various factors related to the diagnosis and treatment of anxiety disorders in women, including medical issues, work and the reproductive cycle, trauma (such as abuse), and marriage and the family. Current research findings indicate that anxiety disorders are three times as common in women as in men. Zerbe points out, however, that truly gender-based research is still in an early stage, so revisions in understanding and treatment are likely. She emphasizes that such advances will benefit men as well.

Robert DuPont notes that after anxiety disorders, addiction to alcohol is the most common mental disorder in the United States. An expanding body of research demonstrates that these two conditions are comorbid about one fourth of the time. Medication plays a substantial role in the treatment of anxiety disorders, whereas psychosocial approaches are more prevalent in addiction treatment. DuPont discusses the danger of construing addiction as "self-medication" for anxiety, particularly in relation to the use of benzodiazepines. Also, failure to distinguish between addicted and nonaddicted anxious persons can lead to underuse of the benzodiazepines for nonaddicted patients and overuse for addicted patients. DuPont concludes with several practical clinical guidelines.

Katherine Shear and Herbert Schulberg point out that although there are reliable diagnostic procedures and effective treatment strategies for patients with anxiety disorders in psychiatric settings, these patients often seek treatment initially from primary care physicians. These providers often do not recognize the disorder and are not trained to treat it. Shear and Schulberg suggest methods for recognizing and treating these conditions more effectively.

In the concluding article, Walter Menninger discusses nine specific challenges to providing integrated treatment of anxiety disorders, the most notable being the factors that affect whether to choose a psychopharmacological, a psychotherapeutic, or an integrated treatment approach. He concludes that more effective dissemination of our increasing knowledge of these disorders may be the most significant challenge to providing integrated treatment.

These papers were written in preparation for a 1995 symposium on "Coping with Anxiety: Integrated Approaches to Treatment," held at the annual meeting of the American Psychiatric Association in Miami, Florida. Both the symposium and this supplement are supported by an unrestricted educational grant from Roche Laboratories, a member of the Roche Group. We extend our sincere thanks to the faculty; to Philip R. Beard, MDiv, MA, managing editor of the *Bulletin of the Menninger Clinic*, for overseeing the planning and publication of the supplement; to the staff of Triclinica Communications, who provided invaluable logistical support; and to our sponsors at Roche Laboratories for making this project possible. Finally, we recognize the extensive assistance of Jon G. Allen, PhD, editor of the *Bulletin of the Menninger Clinic*; the clinicians who served as referees; and the professional editorial staff of the journal, including Mary Ann Clifft, Susan K. Liening, and Laura A. Autrey.

1. Integrated Treatment of Panic Disorder

Jerrold F. Rosenbaum, MD
Rachel A. Pollock, BA
Michael W. Otto, PhD
Mark H. Pollack, MD

Research on the nature and treatment of panic disorder has expanded throughout the past decade with the emergence of new pharmacological strategies and multicomponent cognitive-behavioral interventions. The pharmacopoeia for the treatment of panic disorder has come to include agents of several classes with reported efficacy, including selective serotonin reuptake inhibitors, tricyclic antidepressants, high-potency benzodiazepines, certain anticonvulsants, and others. Cognitive-behavioral strategies now involve treatment components that target the cessation of panic attacks as well as the elimination of anticipatory anxiety and agoraphobic avoidance. Despite the comprehensive effectiveness of these pharmacological and psychosocial interventions, many patients experience residual symptoms, continued impairment, or recurrence. In addition, high rates of Axis I or Axis II comorbidity, extensive avoidance behavior, and other confounding factors may require a comprehensive and integrated therapeutic program, which includes considerations of combination drug therapy and psychosocial interventions.

Clinical characteristics of panic disorder

Panic attacks are characterized by the sudden onset of intense apprehension, fear, or a sense of impending doom. These features, early in the course of the disorder, are typically spontaneous and unexpected, reaching full intensity in 10 minutes or less, and are associated with an array of physical symptoms of autonomic, primarily sympathetic, arousal (American Psychiatric Association, 1994). Epidemiological studies have indicated that approximately 3.5% of the adult United States population meet criteria for panic disorder, an additional 2-5% suffer from agoraphobia with or without panic, and the disorder affects three times as many women as men (Kessler et al., 1994; Myers et al., 1984; Weissman & Merikangas, 1986). Panic disorder usually begins in early adulthood, with many patients reporting a his-

Dr. Rosenbaum is director of the Outpatient Psychiatry Division and chief of the Clinical Psychopharmacology Unit at Massachusetts General Hospital in Boston, where Ms. Pollock is a senior research data analyst, Dr. Otto is director of research, Behavior Therapy Unit, and Dr. Pollack is director of the Anxiety Disorders Program.

tory of clinically significant anxiety dating back to childhood, manifested by separation anxiety, overanxious disorder, school phobia, shyness, or behavioral inhibition in unfamiliar circumstances. In most instances, patients report that the initial or "herald" panic attack is preceded by a significant life event or psychosocial stressor (e.g., a move; a change in relationship, occupation, or job status) (Faravelli, 1985; Roy-Byrne, Uhde, & Post, 1986). The provocative circumstance is often interpreted as a threat to the individual's sense of safety and security in the world, or as a disruption of an established attachment bond; however, physiological stimuli, such as medical illness or substance abuse, may also trigger panic attacks. Once activated, the disorder frequently persists even if the initial stressor is no longer present.

The experience of a panic attack is similar to the fear evoked when a person faces a life-threatening or dangerous situation in which personal security is jeopardized, except that there is no apparent external threat. Intense physiological and psychological arousal is experienced during a panic attack, often along with the impulse to flee that characterizes the fight/flight response. Whether panic disorder does in fact reflect the inappropriate activation of the normal alarm or fight/flight mechanism is a matter for research scrutiny; some evidence suggests that panic has unique features that distinguish it from ordinary fear, such as prominent respiratory symptoms, including sensations of smothering, that are rarely experienced during fear in life-threatening situations (Klein, 1993).

It is presumed that additional factors account for the progression from initial or herald attack to the development of panic disorder. The panic attack itself, although an initial manifestation of disorder, can be viewed as a pathogen also responsible for the subsequent course and complications. A panic attack typically manifests itself in four domains: physical, cognitive, behavioral, and affective. The sudden onset of panic includes an array of *physiological* symptoms: cardiac (chest pain or discomfort, palpitations, tachycardia), respiratory (shortness of breath, choking, smothering sensations), neurological (dizziness, trembling, paresthesias), and gastrointestinal. Accompanying the physical distress is a *cognitive* reaction described as catastrophic misinterpretation, where patients feel an overwhelming sense of terror or a fear of losing control, dying, or going crazy. Varying *behavioral* responses may include the urge to flee the setting of the attack, to seek help, or, alternatively, to "freeze up." Many patients with panic attacks initially seek emergency medical help, convinced they are experiencing a catastrophic medical illness (e.g., a myocardial infarction). *Affectively,* patients will describe a panic attack as the most terrifying event they have ever experienced, and one that they will do almost anything to avoid reexperiencing. Individual panic attacks appear to be fairly common, with one study indicating that as many as 10% of the population may experience a panic episode meeting symptom criteria for a panic attack (Norton, Cox, & Malan, 1992; Norton, Harrison, Hauch, & Rhodes, 1985); only a small percentage of these individuals, however, appear to develop full-blown panic disorder. These findings suggest that in some people, the response to initial panic may play a role in the further progression of the disorder.

Panic disorder, like other Axis I conditions, often occurs against a backdrop of comorbid disorders. For example, in the National Comorbidity Study (Kessler et al., 1994), 56% of respondents (noninstitutionalized civilians from the general population, ages 15-54) with a history of at least one disorder also met criteria for one or more additional disorders. For patients with panic disorder, comorbid psychiatric disorders often include affective disorders, other anxiety disorders, substance abuse, somatization disorders, and personality disorders. For example, Reiter and colleagues (1991) examined comorbidity among patients with panic disorder enrolled in treatment and found that 30% of panic disorder patients had comorbid social phobia, 21% had generalized anxiety disorder, and 1% had obsessive-compulsive disorder; comorbid social phobia was associated with increased rates of depression in these patients. The prevalence of depression in this population overall was also high. One half to two thirds of patients reported past or present major depression, with evidence that depression may emerge in some patients despite ongoing treatment (Ball, Otto, Pollack, & Rosenbaum, 1994; Breier, Charney, & Heninger, 1984). Rates of substance abuse have also been reported to be elevated in patients with anxiety disorders, with one finding indicating that almost one fourth of patients with panic disorder had a history of alcohol dependence. Patients with additional depression or social phobia comorbidity had the higher rates, supporting the idea that self-medication attempts are often coexistent with these disorders (Helzer & Pryzbeck, 1988; Kushner, Sher, & Beitman, 1990; Otto, Pollack, Sachs, O'Neil, & Rosenbaum, 1992).

Rates of Axis II pathology, as assessed by self-report questionnaires, are commonly in the range of 40-70% in patients with panic disorder, with avoidant, borderline, dependent, and histrionic disorders frequently emerging as the most common diagnoses (Diaferia et al., 1993; Mavissakalian, 1990; Pollack, Otto, Rosenbaum, & Sachs, 1992). In addition to increasing the overall distress of patients and providing multiple targets for interventions, comorbid conditions tend to contribute to treatment resistance and symptom maintenance (Fava, Grandi, Saviotti, & Conti, 1990; Keijsers, Hoogduin, & Schaap, 1994; Noyes et al., 1990; Pollack et al., 1990; Reiter et al., 1991; Starcevic, Uhlenhuth, Kellner, & Pathak, 1992).

Overall, the varying presentation of panic disorder and comorbid conditions requires careful diagnosis and selection of interventions. In addition, anxiety disorders must be differentiated from a variety of medical conditions and their treatment that may be associated with significant anxiety symptoms. Disorders such as hyperthyroidism, hypoglycemia, congestive heart failure, cardiac arrhythmias, pheochromocytoma, audiovestibular dysfunctions, complex partial seizures, caffeinism, and the excessive use of bronchodilators or substance abuse may produce panic-like symptoms and complicate the treatment of panic disorder patients (Tesar & Rosenbaum, 1993). The onset of anxiety symptoms after age 40, lack of personal or family history of anxiety disorders, negative history of childhood anxiety, absence of significant life events triggering or worsening anxiety symptoms, lack of avoidance behavior, and poor response to known antipanic agents may all suggest that presenting panic symptoms are related to organic pathology. Treatment should include correction of the underlying medical condition and/or removal of provocative treatment agents.

Pathways to acquisition

Biological models of panic disorder emphasize a constitutional physiological vulnerability for the disorder, whereas behavioral models acknowledge a possible biological diathesis but emphasize the role of learned responses and thinking patterns in maintaining the disorder. Studies on human anxiety have addressed the question of whether some individuals are predisposed to react catastrophically or with excessive fearfulness to stimuli that would seem only mildly challenging to most. Family studies have demonstrated an increased risk of panic disorder in both first-degree and second-degree relatives of panic disorder patients and a higher rate of concordance for panic attacks in monozygotic as compared with dizygotic twin pairs. These findings suggest an underlying genetic component for the disorder (Crowe, Noyes, Pauls, & Slymen, 1983). Genetic studies also suggest that for some persons, the risk for panic disorder may be inherited as a single gene locus, with a multifactorial mode of transmission (Torgersen, 1983). Several studies in primate research (Suomi, 1986; Suomi, Kraemer, Baysinger, & DeLizio, 1981) and preliminary studies of human anxiety (Crowe et al., 1983; Faravelli, 1985; Gittelman & Klein, 1985; Kagan, Reznick, & Snidman, 1987; Raskin, Peeke, Dickman, & Pinsker, 1982; Rosenbaum et al., 1988) support a model of inherited constitutional vulnerability to a lower threshold of limbic arousal to challenge or a model of facilitated sympathetic activation.

Studies of children at risk for anxiety disorders further advance the notion that panic disorder may be one manifestation of an "anxiety proneness." Direct observation of the children of panic disorder and agoraphobia patients reveals high rates of behavioral inhibition to the unfamiliar, a temperamental quality characterized by increased arousal (laboratory-demonstrated increased sympathetic activity), anxiety, and the tendency to withdraw in the face of novel stimuli (Kagan, 1989; Kagan et al., 1987). These inhibited children also demonstrate increased rates of anxiety and depressive disorders, as do their first-degree relatives, which supports the assertion of a familial vulnerability to the development of anxiety disorders. Consistent with these findings, retrospective studies indicate that adult panic disorder patients report having suffered from high rates of childhood anxiety disorders (Gittelman & Klein, 1984, 1985; Klein, 1964; Otto, Pollack, Rosenbaum, Sachs, & Asher, 1994; Pollack, Otto, Sabatino, et al., 1995; Zitrin & Ross, 1988).

Although preliminary, these data, along with parallel findings in animal models (Suomi, 1986; Suomi et al., 1981), suggest a possible anxiety-proneness of these children to react fearfully to normal developmental stressors and to adversity. Such children are more likely than their uninhibited counterparts to manifest fear-like responses when confronted with relevant challenges such as separation, to be vulnerable to adverse developmental experiences such as parental absence or abuse, to require more nurturance and support from the home environment, and, in the absence of adequate developmental buffers, to be vulnerable under stressful life events to the perturbation of this dysregulated system. Presumably, the temperamental characteristic of behavioral inhibition reflects a substrate for interaction between a constitutional vulnerability or diathesis and psychosocial factors, ultimately setting the stage for the evolution of a variety of pathological fears across the life cycle (Rosenbaum et al., 1992; Rosenbaum, Biederman, Hirshfeld, Bolduc, & Chaloff, 1991; Rosenbaum, Biederman, Hirshfeld, Bolduc, Faraone, et al., 1991).

Panic disorder as biological disorder
A strong biological model of panic disorder emphasizes qualitative differences between panic attacks and other types of anxiety. The stereotyped clinical features of panic disorder, including an intense

state of arousal and respiratory distress arising without clear-cut precipitants, are considered neurobiologically distinct from more generalized or anticipatory anxiety. In this view, the disorder is conceptualized as a manifestation of a genetically inherent neurochemical dysfunction (Klein, 1981; Klein, Rabkin, & Gorman, 1985; Sheehan, 1982). Drawing on human and animal models of separation (a normally occurring unlearned alarm reaction that becomes activated by periods of separation from attachment figures), Klein (1981) hypothesized that an innate biological mechanism controls the similar affective responses presenting in panic attacks. An abnormally lowered threshold resulting in active, help-seeking behavior was considered the underlying cause of panic attacks, and such a chronically lowered threshold could become activated even in the absence of significant triggers such as separation. Panic attacks, in this view, are likely to recur as long as the underlying dysfunction persists, thus providing a rationale for the selection and development of treatment interventions that target neurobiological circuits involved in these discharges.

Dysregulation in certain fear-associated central nervous system circuits may be associated with panic disorder. Fear behavior mediated by central nervous system arousal has been linked to central noradrenergic nuclei, particularly the nucleus locus ceruleus (Redmond, Huang, Snyder, & Maas, 1976), which provides most of the brain's norepinephrine. Abnormalities in the brain's noradrenergic system, most likely at the level of the central adrenergic alpha-2 autoreceptor, have been implicated in expression of panic disorder. Positron emission tomography (PET) studies have identified increased metabolic activity in the septohippocampal system in the brains of individuals with lactate-induced panic attacks (Reiman, Raichle, Butler, Herscovitch, & Robins, 1984; Reiman et al., 1986). This brain region is also believed to play a critical role in vigilance and the alarm response (Gray, 1982). Other studies suggest roles for various other factors in the neurobiology of panic disorder. Among them are cortisol-releasing factor; adenosine (Uhde, 1990); a variety of neuropeptides, including cholecystokinin (Bradwejn, 1993); the serotonergic system (Lesch et al., 1992; Woods & Charney, 1988); and central benzodiazepine receptor subsensitivity (Roy-Byrne, Dager, Cowley, Vitaliano, & Dunner, 1989). Support for the medical illness model stems from experimental panic induction by biological probes such as CO_2 inhalation (Woods, Charney, Goodman, & Heninger, 1988), hyperventilation (Gorman et al., 1984), lactate infusion (Liebowitz et al., 1985), caffeine (Charney, Heninger, & Jatlow, 1985), yohimbine (Charney, Heninger, & Breier, 1984), and CCK tetrapeptide (Bradwejn,

Koszycki, & Shrigui, 1991), and successful treatment with pharmacological agents. In this biological model, drug treatment directs therapy toward reregulating this dysregulated physiological system, addresses the underlying constitutional vulnerability, treats or facilitates the treatment of complications, and reduces severe impairment and distress to the point of remission, or to the degree that other therapies become realistic options for patients.

Panic disorder as fear of fear

Cognitive-behavioral models of panic disorder stem from several lines of work (Barlow, 1988; Beck, Emery, & Greenberg, 1985; Clark, 1986; Goldstein & Chambless, 1978; McNally, 1990) proposing that panic disorder is maintained by a "fear-of-fear" cycle in which patients learn to fear the physical symptoms of anxiety and panic. According to these models, catastrophic interpretations of somatic sensations of autonomic arousal (e.g., "I am having a heart attack," "I am going crazy," "I am going to die") cue the activation of fear responses, triggering a panic attack. Initial panic attacks are often viewed as a product of situational stress and/or biological provocation, but recurrent attacks are thought to represent activation of the body's alarm response to danger, motivated by the misinterpretation of symptoms and their perceived consequences. Hence, in the absence of an actual threat, initial autonomic symptoms of arousal are interpreted catastrophically, setting off a cascade of increasing fear and arousal. With recurrent panic attacks, sensitivity to these sensations and the situations that herald them increases. Memories of panic attacks can also serve to maintain a state of hypervigilance to these fearful sensations. Over time, patients may respond automatically with panic to feared sensations without attention to mediating cognitions. Hence, the fear-of-fear cycle is regenerated in a vicious cycle as hypervigilance to somatic sensations ensures that subtle sensations are noticed and in turn catastrophically misinterpreted. Avoidant behavior, conditioned fear reactions, and chronic arousal are additional factors that help perpetuate the fear-of-fear cycle.

Findings from biological provocation studies are generally consistent with this model. Rather than being a product of differences in biological mechanisms existing between panic disorder patients and control subjects, the effects of provocation procedures are hypothesized to occur because patients with panic disorder fear the bodily sensations induced by these procedures. Even though provocation procedures span a wide range of agents and procedures (caffeine, cholecystokinin, isoproterenol, metachlorophenyl piperazine, norepinephrine, sodium lactate, yohimbine, carbon dioxide inhalation, hyperventilation, and exercise), they share the ability to rapidly induce uncomfortable bodily sensations. (For reviews, see McNally, 1994, and Rapee, 1995.) According to the fear-of-fear model of panic disorder, it is the fear and catastrophic interpretation of these sensations and their consequences that is ultimately responsible for the provocation effect. Indeed, manipulations of a subject's perceived controllability of provocation symptoms and the degree to which symptoms are unexpected have been shown to play an important role in some provocation procedures (McNally, 1994). However, the role of fear of anxiety sensations in explaining the provocation effect receives its most direct support from findings demonstrating that individuals who fear anxiety sensations, but who have no history of panic disorder or panic attacks, respond with anxiety and panic to provocation procedures (Donnell & McNally, 1989; Telch & Harrington, 1992). Fear of anxiety symptoms has also been implicated in the genesis and maintenance of panic disorder (Maller & Reiss, 1992; Otto & Gould, in press).

Treatment: The antipanic pharmacopoeia

Several medications have well-documented acute efficacy for the treatment of panic disorder and its complications. These include antidepressive agents (e.g., monoamine oxidase inhibitors, tricyclic antidepressants, selective serotonin reuptake inhibitors), high-potency benzodiazepines (alprazolam and clonazepam), and others. Their efficacy appears to fit with neurobiological models of panic disorder in that these agents regulate locus ceruleus firing and/or limbic system activity (Grant, Huang, & Redmond, 1980). The psychopharmacology of panic disorder has been extensively reviewed elsewhere (Lydiard, 1988; Rosenbaum, 1990; Rosenbaum & Gelenberg, 1991); this section will briefly describe frequently used agents, noting clinically relevant issues, problems, and strategies to increase treatment effectiveness.

Tricyclic antidepressants
The tricyclic antidepressants (TCAs) were the first pharmacological agents noted to be effective for the treatment of panic disorder (Klein, 1964). Since then, many controlled trials have demonstrated the efficacy of these agents, which include imipramine, desipramine, and nortriptyline. The mechanism of action of these agents in panic disorder is uncertain; however, the regulation of subsensitive alpha-2 autoreceptors has been proposed to be potentially relevant (Charney & Heninger, 1985). The time to therapeutic onset with antidepressants is typically at least 3-4 weeks. During initiation of TCA treat-

ment, patients may experience marked increases in anxiety, panic, and jitteriness; thus a low starting dose is recommended (e.g., 10 mg/day "test dose" imipramine), titrated as tolerated in 25 mg increments up to doses of 100-300 mg/day. Adverse effects may include cardiac disturbances, orthostatic hypotension, anticholinergic effects (dry mouth, blurred vision, constipation), weight gain, sexual dysfunction, and, as noted, early worsening of anxiety, all of which may reduce treatment compliance (Noyes, Garvey, Cook, & Samuelson, 1989).

Although less commonly used for this indication in the United States, the TCA clomipramine (also a serotonin reuptake inhibitor) may be more effective for some panic disorder patients than imipramine (Modigh, Westberg, & Eriksson, 1992). Although side effects may limit clomipramine's use, some patients may respond to relatively low doses (e.g., 25-50 mg/day).

Monoamine oxidase inhibitors

Monoamine oxidase inhibitors (MAOIs), such as phenelzine, tranylcypromine, and isocarboxazid, have demonstrated efficacy for the treatment of panic disorder. This drug class is considered by some clinicians to include the most comprehensively effective agents for treating panic disorder, blocking panic attacks and relieving depression (particularly atypical symptoms) and concomitant social anxiety (Sheehan, Ballenger, & Jacobsen, 1980). Recommended dose ranges are 45-90 mg/day for phenelzine and 30-60 mg/day for tranylcypromine. The use of MAOIs is limited by their association with adverse effects, including orthostatic hypotension, weight gain, and insomnia. In addition, the need for careful dietary monitoring and risk of hypertensive crisis may make their use daunting for many patients. Thus MAOIs are often reserved for nonresponders to safer and better tolerated drugs.

In light of these obstacles, moclobemide and brofaromine, reversible inhibitors of the monoamine oxidase A enzyme, have been used successfully for the treatment of social phobia and panic disorder (Van Vliet, Westenberg, & Den-Boer, 1993; Versiani et al., 1992). Although not available in the United States, these agents have proven beneficial for the treatment of anxiety disorders, with a markedly decreased risk of the serious adverse effects associated with the older, nonselective MAOIs.

Selective serotonin reuptake inhibitors

As a result of their efficacy, safety, and generally favorable side-effect profiles, the selective serotonin reuptake inhibitors (SSRIs) have been widely accepted as first-line treatment of depression and other disorders. After showing favorable clinical response in panic disorder patients (Den-Boer & Westenberg, 1990; Gorman et al., 1987), these agents are now being subjected to controlled studies in anxiety disorder patients (Goddard et al., 1993; Schneier et al., 1990). The SSRIs are suitable as first-line treatment for panic disorder, especially where comorbid depression is present. To minimize increased anxiety and "jitteriness," treatment may be initiated with a low dose (e.g., fluoxetine 5-10 mg) and gradually titrated up to typical doses over the first few weeks. Typical SSRI-associated side effects include gastrointestinal distress, headaches, sleep disturbance, and sexual dysfunction; overall, however, these agents are well tolerated by most patients. The benign cardiovascular profile of the SSRIs also makes them a more attractive pharmacological option for patients with cardiac pathology or for those markedly sensitive to cardiac symptoms (such as tachycardia) induced by other antidepressants.

Benzodiazepines

High-potency benzodiazepines, such as clonazepam, alprazolam, and lorazepam, have been reported to be effective for blocking panic attacks, along with their known efficacy for controlling generalized anxiety. The advantages of a benzodiazepine for this syndrome include rapid onset of therapeutic effect and a safe, favorable side-effect profile. The triazolobenzodiazepine alprazolam has undergone extensive study for the treatment of panic disorder (Ballenger et al., 1988; "Cross-National Collaborative Panic Study," 1992). The starting dose of alprazolam is generally 0.5 mg twice a day, titrating to a maintenance dose between 2 and 10 mg daily. Symptoms of ataxia and drowsiness at treatment initiation, when present, are usually transient.

Potential drawbacks of the benzodiazepines, particularly shorter acting ones such as alprazolam, include concerns about abuse and dependency, withdrawal symptoms on abrupt discontinuation, early relapse on discontinuation, and interdose rebound anxiety. The interdose rebound may exacerbate patients' concerns about panic; it necessitates frequent dosing (typically four times a day), which from a cognitive-behavioral perspective may be counterproductive because it focuses patients on the link between anxiolysis and pill taking. These complications suggest the advantage of a longer lasting agent, such as clonazepam.

Clonazepam, another high-potency benzodiazepine, has also been used with success as an antipanic agent (Pollack, Rosenbaum, Tesar, Herman, & Sachs, 1987; Tesar et al., 1991). Its long duration of effect diminishes the need for multiple daily dosing. Initial low doses (e.g., 0.25 mg/day) are gradually titrated to the usual effective dose (1-5 mg/day). Symptoms of initial sedation and ataxia are also usually transient. Benzodiazepines are not generally abused by patients with panic disorder; in fact, they are usually underutilized rather than overused (Clinthorne, Cisin, Balter, Mellinger, & Uhlenhuth, 1986; Mellinger, Balter, & Uhlenhuth, 1984; Pollack, Otto, Kaspi, Hammerness, & Rosenbaum, 1994). The use of benzodiazepines with patients with panic who also have a history of substance abuse or dependence is usually reserved for those whose suffering was not ameliorated by other agents or strategies.

Treatment-emergent depression may complicate benzodiazepine therapy in a minority (10%) of panic disorder patients (Cohen & Rosenbaum, 1987). These patients with comorbid depression or a strong personal or family history of depression should generally receive antidepressants as part of their pharmacotherapy regimen.

Other agents
Other antidepressants, such as bupropion, trazodone, and amoxapine, appear relatively ineffective for the treatment of panic disorder. Beta blockers, such as propranolol, do not specifically block the cognitive fear experience of panic and are thus not used as primary treatments for panic disorder, although they adjunctively reduce associated physical symptoms such as tachycardia and tremor. Clonidine, an alpha-2 receptor agonist that decreases locus ceruleus firing, has demonstrated initial improvement in panic disorder patients, although the benefits tend not to be maintained (Liebowitz, Fyer, McGrath, & Klein, 1981; Uhde et al., 1989). In a case series, Gastfriend and Rosenbaum (1989) described four partial responders to other antipanic treatment regimens whose therapy was augmented by the addition of the nonbenzodiazepine anxiolytic buspirone; beneficial doses were in the range of 30-60 mg/day. Among the nonbenzodiazepine anticonvulsants, valproic acid has proven efficacious for typical, atypical, and treatment-resistant panic disorder patients (Keck, Taylor, Tugrul, McElroy, & Bennett, 1993).

Pharmacotherapy treatment outcomes

Efficacy, as measured by panic-free rates, from a single pharmacological treatment trial with either an antidepressant or a benzodiazepine in panic disorder patients is reported in the review literature to range from 50% to 70% ("Cross-National Collaborative Panic Study," 1992; Tesar et al., 1991). Meta-analytic techniques that make use of standardized scores (effect sizes) allow for comparisons across these studies, and specific outcome measures. In a recently completed meta-analysis, Gould, Otto, and Pollack (1995) found that effect sizes for both benzodiazepine and antidepressant treatments were higher than placebo. Although when compared to each other the two treatments did not differ significantly, antidepressants did achieve a subtle advantage over benzodiazepines (effect size = 0.55 vs. 0.40). Antidepressant treatments also had a higher dropout rate (25.4%) than did benzodiazepines (13.1%), supporting reports in the literature regarding the more favorable side-effect profile of the benzodiazepine agents (Charney & Heninger, 1986; Pollack & Rosenbaum, 1988).

It is important to note that in acute controlled trials, 30-75% of patients continued to experience panic attacks and/or residual phobic avoidance (Ballenger et al., 1988; "Cross-National Collaborative Panic Study," 1992; Tesar et al., 1991). Many patients may require ongoing medication treatments and may remain symptomatic despite ongoing treatment. Findings from longitudinal assessments of 1.5-6 years after medication initiation indicate that 50-80% of patients remained symptomatic with sustained anxiety difficulties, while 40% continued to experience some panic attacks (Nagy, Krystal, Woods, & Charney, 1989; Noyes, Garvey, & Cook, 1989; Pollack et al., 1993). For patients on benzodiazepines, some slippage in acute efficacy over the long term may be associated with dose reduction over time (Pollack et al., 1993). Intriguing data from Mavissakalian and Perel (1992) suggest that patients in remission after acute TCA treatment with imipramine may tolerate dose reduction without loss of acute treatment gains. Adjunctive behavioral therapy may improve long-term outcome of pharmacologically treated patients.

Relapse is common when pharmacotherapy is discontinued, and is consistent with the notion that panic disorder is not a discrete disorder (i.e., with a specific onset and offset and a predetermined course and treatment plan). Although these effects have been reported with antidepressants (Noyes, Garvey, & Cook, 1989), discontinuation difficulties are often more acute with the high-potency benzodiazepines. Emergent problems associated with the discontinuation of pharmacological treatment include the inability to successfully complete taper programs and the return of panic and severe symptoms in some patients (Fyer et al., 1987; Noyes, Garvey, & Cook, 1989), thus leaving some patients on medication for extended periods. In some cases, long-term treatment may serve primarily to prevent the onset of discontinuation symptoms. Benzodiazepine taper may be associated with symptoms that mimic the symptoms of anxiety and panic, making the patient fearful of and, in the cognitive-behavioral model, susceptible to panic attack recurrence (Otto, Pollack, Sachs, et al., 1993). Gradual taper with the high-potency benzodiazepines and antidepressants is critical to maximize the likelihood of successful taper (Rickels, Schweizer, Weiss, & Zavodnick, 1993). Adjunctive treatment with cognitive-behavioral therapy may address an underlying anxiety sensitivity through exposure to feared somatic sensations and facilitate a successful benzodiazepine taper (Otto, Pollack, Meltzer-Brody, & Rosenbaum, 1993). In a recent study by Otto, Pollack, Meltzer-Brody, and Rosenbaum (1993), 76% of patients who received cognitive-behavioral therapy while tapering successfully completed benzodiazepine discontinuation, compared to only 25% of those experiencing a slow taper alone.

Treatment: Cognitive-behavioral therapy

In contrast to the view that panic disorder is a chronic condition requiring ongoing medication treatment, cognitive-behavioral practitioners argue that cognitive-behavioral therapy (CBT) offers an alternative, highly effective treatment option, even for complicated cases of panic. Throughout the 1970s, cognitive-behavioral treatments tended to emphasize the treatment of the agoraphobic avoidance accompanying panic disorder rather than of the manifestations of the panic attacks themselves. In the 1980s, however, additional treatments were developed that directly targeted panic attacks and the fear-of-fear cycle hypothesized to underlie panic disorder (Barlow, 1988; Clark, 1986). Current cognitive-behavioral treatments for panic disorder often emphasize five treatment components: (1) information on the nature of panic disorder and the fear-of-fear cycle, (2) the acquisition of symptom management skills, including relaxation training and diaphragmatic breathing, (3) cognitive restructuring and the elimination of catastrophic misinterpretation of anxiety symptoms, (4) interoceptive exposure aimed at eliminating the fear of anxiety sensations through a process of stepwise exposure to these particular symptoms, and (5) in vivo exposure aimed at eliminating the avoidance that accompanies anxiety disorders.

Studies of treatments using these components have reported high rates of success. In recent trials, panic-free rates ranging from 71-87% for short-term treatment have been reported (Barlow, Craske, Cerny, & Klosko, 1989; Beck, Sokol, Clark, Berchick, & Wright, 1992; Clark et al., 1994; Klosko, Barlow, Tassinari, & Cerny, 1990; Margraf, Barlow, Clark, & Telch, 1993). The efficacy of these most recent strategies is also associated with high rates of maintenance of treatment gains. For example, Craske, Brown, and Barlow (1991) found that at 2-year follow-up, approximately 80% of patients remained panic free. Similar rates were found at 1-year follow-up periods in other studies (Beck et al., 1992; Margraf et al., 1993). Crossover of patients to cognitive-behavioral therapy after they have failed to respond to supportive psychotherapy also supports the efficacy of this intervention (Beck et al., 1992). In addition, CBT has been found to benefit treatment-resistent patients receiving medication alone (Pollack et al., 1994) and has served to augment response and maintenance of acute benzodiazepine treatment (Hegel, Ravaris, & Ahles, 1994; Spiegel, Bruce, Gregg, & Nuzzarello, 1994). In addition to the use of CBT as a first-line intervention for panic disorder, its success argues for the application of exposure and cognitive restructuring procedures in patients failing to respond or responding incompletely to pharmacological interventions, those who frequently experience relapse, and those attempting discontinuation of pharmacotherapy.

In the meta-analytic studies comparing controlled trials of either pharmacotherapy or behavior therapy for panic disorder, cognitive-behavioral treatments routinely perform as well as pharmacotherapy (Clum, Clum, & Surls, 1993; Gould et al., 1995), although patient self-selection or other sample differences may account for differences in outcomes across CBT and drug studies. As noted by Gould and colleagues (1995), cognitive-behavioral treatments have also been associated with high rates of retention in treatment, and, in many cases, with a superior cost/benefit ratio.

Choice of treatment

There is ongoing debate about whether most panic disorder patients should be treated initially with cognitive-behavioral or pharmacological approaches for the management of panic disorder. Cognitive-behavioral therapists view CBT as the treatment of first choice, whereas many psychopharmacologists argue that the suppression of the panic with medication is often sufficient to eliminate secondary phobic avoidance without specifically targeted therapy (Otto & Pollack, 1994). Other studies have found that the addition of exposure improves the outcome of medication treatment (Mavissakalian & Michelson, 1986; Telch, Agras, Taylor, Roth, & Gallen, 1985). In practice, the concurrent administration of cognitive-behavioral and pharmacological therapies may also result in less medication than if treating with medication alone (Charney & Heninger, 1985, 1986; Charney et al., 1986).

CBT may offer some patients with panic disorder and agoraphobia the potential for good acute outcome and long-term maintenance of treatment gains without the need for ongoing medication treatment or the exposure to drug-related side effects or discontinuation difficulties; however, the treatment does require an investment of time and effort to be successful. By their nature, pharmacological interventions offer good acute outcome with a minimum of time devoted to treatment. It is not clear, though, whether concurrent medication treatment significantly improves the outcome of CBT. There is limited evidence that short-term pharmacological treatment may interfere with the effects of exposure treatment (Marks et al., 1993), although it appears that under the right conditions, medication can be added to CBT without loss of efficacy (Otto, Gould, & Pollack, 1994).

Additional studies underway (Barlow, Gorman, Shear, & Woods, study in progress) may provide important information about relative indications for pharmacotherapy and CBT alone or in combination. For instance, while pharmacological trials may employ fixed or flexible blind-dose strategies with single agents, clinicians in practice often use combination treatment (e.g., SSRIs alone or in combination with high-potency benzodiazepines such as clonazepam) openly titrated according to individual patient adaptation to adverse effects and to response. In addition, polypharmacy offers the potential for improving on the outcome documented in single-agent studies of efficacy, allowing the clinician to maximize the impact of pharmacological strategies.

Whether patients in treatment by physicians are the same, in terms of severity and comorbidity, as those in blinded randomized studies is also open to question. Patients in psychotherapy studies are unblinded to their treatment condition and may have come to particular treatment settings with expectations about *efficacy*. Patient preference for initial treatment for panic disorder is often determined by preconceived notions or specific concerns about the time and process involved in "talking therapy" or the potential adverse effects or social stigma of "taking drugs," such that patients may often be unwilling to consider another treatment modality as long as their preferred treatment is available. An ongoing naturalistic study at the Massachusetts General Hospital hopes to resolve these uncertainties by making available both pharmacotherapy and CBT experts. Patients without a strong preference for CBT or pharmacotherapy are randomized to a treatment modality. Those with a preference receive initial treatment with their choice of intervention. This study will examine the effectiveness of treatment intervention as typically used in a broad spectrum of patients in the general clinical setting and the impact of patient preference on treatment outcome. Patients over time often receive a combination of sequential treatments and are also reassured that choices are available regarding treatment options.

Patients who fail to respond to a full trial of one modality can be referred for an alternative treatment.

Implications for practice and integrated treatment

An integrated model predicts risk for manifest anxiety disorder as a consequence of constitutional vulnerability shaped by developmental experience and activated or influenced by environmental factors. Clinicians should recognize the variable expressions of panic disorder and select intervention strategies that will address evident factors in the etiology, symptomatology, comorbidity, medical and physiological status, and psychosocial influences specific to each patient. For some patients, symptoms may be dramatically alleviated, even after years of distress, through pharmacological or cognitive-behavioral treatments. For other patients, optimal therapeutic outcome may require combination or sustained treatment that addresses the complex interacting physiological, psychosocial, intrapsychic, and interpersonal forces complicating the clinical picture.

In conclusion, there is a wide variety of pharmacological and nonpharmacological interventions that have demonstrated efficacy in treating panic disorder. Thoughtful application of the available therapies alone or in combination may enable patients who have been impaired for years to compensate for a constitutional vulnerability to anxiety, experience resolution of disabling distress, and regain confidence in their ability to function in society.

References

American Psychiatric Association. (1994). *Diagnostic and statistical manual of mental disorders* (4th ed.). Washington DC: Author.

Ball, S.G., Otto, M.W., Pollack, M.H., & Rosenbaum, J.F. (1994). Predicting prospective episodes of depression in patients with panic disorder: A longitudinal study. *Journal of Consulting and Clinical Psychology, 62,* 359-365.

Ballenger, J.C., Burrows, G.D., DuPont, R.L., Jr., Lesser, I.M., Noyes, R., Jr., Pecknold, J.C, Rifkin, A., & Swinson, R.P. (1988). Alprazolam in panic disorder and agoraphobia: Results from a multicenter trial: I. Efficacy in short-term treatment. *Archives of General Psychiatry, 45,* 413-422.

Barlow, D.H. (1988). *Anxiety and its disorders: The nature and treatment of anxiety and panic.* New York: Guilford.

Barlow, D.H., Craske, M.G., Cerny, J.A., & Klosko, J.S. (1989). Behavioral treatment of panic disorder. *Behavior Therapy, 20,* 261-282.

Beck, A.T., Emery, G., & Greenberg, R. (1985). *Anxiety disorders and phobias: A cognitive perspective.* New York: Basic Books.

Beck, A.T., Sokol, L., Clark, D., Berchick, R., & Wright, F. (1992). A crossover study of focused cognitive therapy for panic disorder. *American Journal of Psychiatry, 149,* 778-783.

Bradwejn, J. (1993). Neurobiological investigations into the role of cholecystokinin in panic disorder. *Journal of Psychiatry and Neuroscience, 18,* 178-188.

Bradwejn, J., Koszycki, D., & Shrigui, C. (1991). Enhanced sensitivity to cholecystokinin tetrapeptide in panic disorder: Clinical and behavioral findings. *Archives of General Psychiatry, 48,* 603-610.

Breier, A., Charney, D.S., & Heninger, G.R. (1984). Major depression in patients with agoraphobia and panic attacks. *Archives of General Psychiatry, 41,* 1129-1135.

Charney, D.S., & Heninger, G.R. (1985). Noradrenergic function and the mechanism of action of antianxiety treatment: II. The effect of long-term imipramine treatment. *Archives of General Psychiatry, 42,* 473-481.

Charney, D.S., & Heninger, G.R. (1986). Abnormal regulation of noradrenergic function in panic disorders: Effects of clonidine in healthy subjects and patients with agoraphobia and panic disorder. *Archives of General Psychiatry, 43,* 1042-1054.

Charney, D.S., Heninger, G.R., & Breier, A. (1984). Noradrenergic function in panic anxiety: Effects of yohimbine in healthy subjects and patients with agoraphobia and panic disorder. *Archives of General Psychiatry, 41,* 751-763.

Charney, D.S., Heninger, G.R., & Jatlow, P.I. (1985). Increased anxiogenic effects of caffeine in panic disorders. *Archives of General Psychiatry, 42,* 233-243.

Charney, D.S., Woods, S.W., Goodman, W.K., Rifkin, B., Kinch, M., Aiken, B., Quadrino, L.M., & Heninger, G.R. (1986). Drug treatment of panic disorder: The comparative efficacy of imipramine, alprazolam, and trazodone. *Journal of Clinical Psychiatry, 47,* 580-586.

Clark, D.M. (1986). A cognitive approach to panic. *Behaviour Research and Therapy, 24,* 461-470.

Clark, D.M., Salkovskis, P.M., Hackmann, A., Middleton, H., Pavlos, A., & Gelder, M. (1994). A comparison of cognitive therapy, applied relaxation and imipramine in the treatment of panic disorder. *British Journal of Psychiatry, 164,* 759-769.

Clinthorne, J.K., Cisin, I.H., Balter, M.B., Mellinger, G.D., & Uhlenhuth, E.H. (1986). Changes in popular attitudes and beliefs about tranquilizers: 1970-1979. *Archives of General Psychiatry, 43,* 527-532.

Clum, G.A., Clum, G.A., & Surls, R. (1993). A meta-analysis of treatments for panic disorder. *Journal of Consulting and Clinical Psychology, 61,* 317-326.

Cohen, L.S., & Rosenbaum, J.F. (1987). Clonazepam: New uses and potential problems. *Journal of Clinical Psychiatry, 48*(10, Suppl.), 50-55.

Craske, M.G., Brown, T.A., & Barlow, D.H. (1991). Behavioral treatment of panic disorder: A two-year follow-up. *Behavior Therapy, 22,* 289-304.

Cross-National Collaborative Panic Study, Second Phase Investigators. (1992). Drug treatment of panic disorder: Comparative efficacy of alprazolam, imipramine, and placebo. *British Journal of Psychiatry, 160,* 191-202.

Crowe, R.R., Noyes, R., Pauls, D.L., & Slymen, D. (1983). A family study of panic disorder. *Archives of General Psychiatry, 40,* 1065-1069.

Den-Boer, J.A., & Westenberg, H.G. (1990). Serotonin function in panic disorder: A double blind placebo controlled study with fluvoxamine and ritanserin. *Psychopharmacology, 102,* 85-94.

Diaferia, G., Sciuto, G., Perna, G., Bernardeschi, L., Battaglia, M., Rusmini, S., & Bellodi, L. (1993). DSM-III-R personality disorders in panic disorder. *Journal of Anxiety Disorders, 7,* 153-161.

Donnell, C.D., & McNally, R.J. (1989). Anxiety sensitivity and history of panic as predictors of response to hyperventilation. *Behaviour Research and Therapy, 28,* 83-85.

Faravelli, C. (1985). Life events preceding the onset of panic disorder. *Journal of Affective Disorders, 9,* 103-105.

Fava, G.A., Grandi, S., Saviotti, F.M., & Conti, S. (1990). Hypochondriasis with panic attacks. *Psychosomatics, 31,* 351-353.

Fyer, A.J., Liebowitz, M.R., Gorman, J.M., Campeas, R., Levin, A., Davies, S.O., Goetz, D., & Klein, D.F. (1987). Discontinuation of alprazolam treatment in panic patients. *American Journal of Psychiatry, 144,* 303-308.

Gastfriend, D.R., & Rosenbaum, J.F. (1989). Adjunctive buspirone in benzodiazepine treatment of four patients with panic disorder. *American Journal of Psychiatry, 146,* 914-916.

Gittelman, R., & Klein, D.F. (1984). Relationship between separation anxiety and panic and agoraphobic disorders. *Psychopathology, 17*(Suppl. 1), 56-65.

Gittelman, R., & Klein, D.F. (1985). Childhood separation anxiety and adult agoraphobia. In A.H. Tuma & J. Maser (Eds.), *Anxiety and the anxiety disorders* (pp. 389-402). Hillsdale, NJ: Erlbaum.

Goddard, A.W., Woods, S.W., Sholomskas, D.E., Goodman, W.K., Charney, D.S., & Heninger, G.R. (1993). Effects of the serotonin reuptake inhibitor fluvoxamine on yohimbine-induced anxiety in panic disorder. *Psychiatry Research, 48,* 119-133.

Goldstein, A.J., & Chambless, D.L. (1978). A reanalysis of agoraphobia. *Behavior Therapy, 9*(1), 47-59.

Gorman, J.M., Askanazi, J., Liebowitz, M.R., Fyer, A.J., Stein, J., Kinney, J.M., & Klein, D.F. (1984). Response to hyperventilation in a group of patients with panic disorder. *American Journal of Psychiatry, 141,* 857-861.

Gorman, J.M., Liebowitz, M.R., Fyer, A.J., Goetz, D., Campeas, R.B., Ryer, M.R., Davies, S.O., & Klein, D.F. (1987). An open trial of fluoxetine in the treatment of panic attacks. *Journal of Clinical Psychopharmacology, 7,* 329-332.

Gould, R.A., Otto, M.W., & Pollack, M.H. (1995). *A meta-analysis of treatment outcome for panic disorder.* Manuscript submitted for publication.

Grant, S.J., Huang, Y.H., & Redmond, D.E. (1980). Benzodiazepines attenuate single unit activity in the locus coeruleus. *Life Sciences, 27,* 2231-2236.

Gray, J.A. (1982). *The neuropsychology of anxiety: An inquiry into the functions of the septo-hippocampal system.* New York: Oxford University Press.

Hegel, M.T., Ravaris, C.L., & Ahles, T.A. (1994). Combined cognitive-behavioral and time-limited alprazolam treatment of panic disorder. *Behavior Therapy, 25,* 183-195.

Helzer, J.E., & Pryzbeck, T.R. (1988). The co-occurrence of alcoholism with other psychiatric disorders in the general population and its impact on treatment. *Journal of Studies on Alcohol, 49,* 219-224.

Kagan, J. (1989). The concept of behavioral inhibition to the unfamiliar. In J.S. Reznick (Ed.), *Perspectives on behavioral inhibition* (pp. 1-23). Chicago: University of Chicago Press.

Kagan, J., Reznick, J.S., & Snidman, N. (1987). The physiology and psychology of behavioral inhibition in children. *Child Development, 58,* 1459-1473.

Keck, P.E., Jr., Taylor, V.E., Tugrul, K.C., McElroy, S.L., & Bennett, J.A. (1993). Valproate treatment of panic disorder and lactate-induced panic attacks. *Biological Psychiatry, 33,* 542-546.

Keijsers, G.P., Hoogduin, C.A., & Schaap, C.P. (1994). Prognostic factors in the behavioral treatment of panic disorder with and without agoraphobia. *Behavior Therapy, 25,* 689-708.

Kessler, R.C., McGonagle, K.A., Zhao, S., Nelson, C.B., Hughes, M., Eshleman, S., Wittchen, H.-U., & Kendler, K.S. (1994). Lifetime and 12-month prevalence of DSM-III-R psychiatric disorders in the United States: Results from the National Comorbidity Study. *Archives of General Psychiatry, 51,* 8-19.

Klein, D.F. (1964). Delineation of two-drug responsive anxiety syndromes. *Psychopharmacologia, 5,* 397-408.

Klein, D.F. (1981). Anxiety reconceptualized. In D.F. Klein & J.G. Rabkin (Eds.), *Anxiety: New research and changing concepts* (pp. 235-263). New York: Raven.

Klein, D.F. (1993). False suffocation alarms, spontaneous panics, and related conditions: An integrative hypothesis. *Archives of General Psychiatry, 50,* 306-317.

Klein, D.F., Rabkin, J.G., & Gorman, J.M. (1985). Etiological and pathophysiological inferences from the pharmacological treatment of anxiety. In A.H. Tuma & J.D. Maser (Eds.), *Anxiety and the anxiety disorders* (pp. 501-532). Hillsdale, NJ: Erlbaum.

Klosko, J.S., Barlow, D.H., Tassinari, R., & Cerny, J.A. (1990). A comparison of alprazolam and behavior therapy in the treatment of panic disorder. *Journal of Consulting and Clinical Psychology, 58,* 77-84.

Kushner, M.G., Sher, K.J., & Beitman, B.D. (1990). The relation between alcohol problems and the anxiety disorders. *American Journal of Psychiatry, 147,* 685-695.

Lesch, K.P., Weismann, M., Hoh, A., Muller, T., Disselkamp-Tietze, J., Osterheider, M., & Schulte, H.M. (1992). 5-HT 1A receptor-effector system responsivity in panic disorder. *Psychopharmacology, 106,* 111-117.

Liebowitz, M.R., Fyer, A.J., McGrath, P., & Klein, D.F. (1981). Clonidine treatment of panic disorder. *Psychopharmacology Bulletin, 17*(3), 122-123.

Liebowitz, M.R., Gorman, J.M., Fyer, A.J., Levitt, M., Dillon, D., Levy, G., Appleby, I.L., Anderson, S., Palij, M., Davies, S.O., & Klein, D.F. (1985). Lactate provocation of panic attacks: II. Biochemical and physiological findings. *Archives of General Psychiatry, 42,* 709-719.

Lydiard, R.B. (1988). Panic disorder: Pharmacological treatment. *Psychiatric Annals, 18,* 468-472.

Maller, R.G., & Reiss, S. (1992). Anxiety sensitivity in 1984 and panic attacks in 1987. *Journal of Anxiety Disorders, 6,* 241-247.

Margraf, J., Barlow, D.H., Clark, D.M., & Telch, M.J. (1993). Psychological treatment of panic: Work in progress on outcome, active ingredients, and follow-up. *Behaviour Research and Therapy, 31,* 1-8.

Marks, I.M., Swinson, R.P., Basoglu, M., Kuch, K., Noshirvani, H., O'Sullivan, G., Lelliot, P.T., Kirby, M., McNamee, G., Sengun, S., & Wickwire, K. (1993). Alprazolam and exposure alone and combined in panic disorder with agoraphobia: A controlled study in London and Toronto. *British Journal of Psychiatry, 162,* 776-787.

Mavissakalian, M. (1990). The relationship between panic disorder/agoraphobia and personality disorders. *Psychiatric Clinics of North America, 13,* 664-684.

Mavissakalian, M., & Michelson, L. (1986). Agoraphobia: Relative and combined effectiveness of therapist-assisted *in vivo* exposure and imipramine. *Journal of Clinical Psychiatry, 47,* 117-122.

Mavissakalian, M., & Perel, J. (1992). Clinical experiments in maintenance and discontinuation of imipramine therapy in panic disorder with agoraphobia. *Archives of General Psychiatry, 49,* 318-323.

McNally, R.J. (1990). Psychological approaches to panic disorder: A review. *Psychological Bulletin, 108,* 403-419.

McNally, R.J. (1994). *Panic disorder: A critical analysis.* New York: Guilford.

Mellinger, G.D., Balter, M.B., & Uhlenhuth, E.H. (1984). Prevalence and correlates of the long-term regular use of anxiolytics. *Journal of the American Medical Association, 251,* 375-379.

Modigh, K., Westberg, P., & Eriksson, E. (1992). Superiority of clomipramine over imipramine in the treatment of panic disorder: A placebo-controlled trial. *Journal of Clinical Psychopharmacology, 12,* 251-261.

Myers, J.K., Weissman, M.M., Tischler, G.L., Holzer, C.E., III, Leaf, P.J., Orvaschel, H., Anthony, J.C., Boyd, J.H., Burke, J.D., Jr., Kramer, M., & Stoltzman, R. (1984). Six-month prevalence of psychiatric disorders in three communities: 1980-1982. *Archives of General Psychiatry, 41,* 959-967.

Nagy, L.M., Krystal, J.H., Woods, S.W., & Charney, D.S. (1989). Clinical and medication outcome after short-term alprazolam and behavioral group treatment in panic disorder: 2.5-year naturalistic follow-up study. *Archives of General Psychiatry, 46,* 993-999.

Norton, G.R., Cox, B.J., & Malan, J. (1992). Nonclinical panickers: A critical review. *Clinical Psychology Review, 12,* 121-139.

Norton, G.R., Harrison, B., Hauch, J., & Rhodes, L. (1985). Characteristics of people with infrequent panic attacks. *Journal of Abnormal Psychology, 94,* 216-221.

Noyes, R., Jr., Garvey, M.J., & Cook, B.L. (1989). Follow-up study of patients with panic disorder and agoraphobia with panic attacks treated with tricyclic antidepressants. *Journal of Affective Disorders, 16,* 249-257.

Noyes, R., Garvey, M.J., Cook, B.L., & Samuelson, L. (1989). Problems with tricyclic antidepressant use in patients with panic disorder or agoraphobia: Results of a naturalistic follow-up study. *Journal of Clinical Psychiatry, 50,* 163-169.

Noyes, R., Reich, J., Christiansen, J., Suelzer, M., Pfohl, B., & Coryell, W.A. (1990). Outcome of panic disorder: Relationship to diagnostic subtypes and comorbidity. *Archives General Psychiatry, 47,* 809-818.

Otto, M.W., & Gould, R.A. (in press). Cognitive-behavior therapy for anxiety disorders: I. Treatment strategies and outcome for panic disorder. In M.H. Pollack, M.W. Otto, & J.F. Rosenbaum (Eds.), *Challenges in psychiatric treatment: Pharmacologic and psychosocial perspectives.* New York: Guilford.

Otto, M.W., Gould, R.A., & Pollack, M.H. (1994). Cognitive-behavioral treatment of panic disorder: Considerations for the treatment of patients over the long term. *Psychiatric Annals, 24,* 307-315.

Otto, M.W., & Pollack, M.H. (1994). Treatment strategies for panic disorder: A debate. *Harvard Review of Psychiatry, 2,* 166-170.

Otto, M.W., Pollack, M.H., Meltzer-Brody, S., & Rosenbaum, J.F. (1993). Cognitive-behavioral therapy for benzodiazepine discontinuation in panic disorder patients. *Psychopharmacology Bulletin, 28,* 123-130.

Otto, M.W., Pollack, M.H., Rosenbaum, J.F., Sachs, G.S., & Asher, R.H. (1994). Childhood history of anxiety in adults with panic disorder: Association with anxiety sensitivity and comorbidity. *Harvard Review of Psychiatry, 1,* 288-293.

Otto, M.W., Pollack, M.H., Sachs, G.S., O'Neil, C.A., & Rosenbaum, J.F. (1992). Alcohol dependence in panic disorder patients. *Journal of Psychiatry Research, 26,* 29-38.

Otto, M.W., Pollack, M.H., Sachs, G.S., Reiter, S.R., Meltzer-Brody, S., & Rosenbaum, J.F. (1993). Discontinuation of benzodiazepine treatment: Efficacy of cognitive-behavioral therapy for patients with panic disorder. *American Journal of Psychiatry, 150,* 1485-1490.

Pollack, M.H., Otto, M.W., Kaspi, S.P., Hammerness, P.G., & Rosenbaum, J.F. (1994). Cognitive behavior therapy for treatment-refractory panic disorder. *Journal of Clinical Psychiatry, 55,* 200-205.

Pollack, M.H., Otto, M.W., Rosenbaum, J.F., & Sachs, G.S. (1992). Personality disorders in patients with panic disorder: Association with childhood anxiety disorders, early trauma, comorbidity, and chronicity. *Comprehensive Psychiatry, 33*(2), 78-83.

Pollack, M.H., Otto, M.W., Rosenbaum, J.F., Sachs, G.S., O'Neil, C., Asher, R., & Meltzer-Brody, S. (1990). Longitudinal course of panic disorder: Findings from the Massachusetts General Hospital Naturalistic Study. *Journal of Clinical Psychiatry, 51*(12, Suppl. A), 12-16.

Pollack, M.H., Otto, M.W., Sabatino, S., Majcher, D., Worthington, J.J., McArdle, E.T., & Rosenbaum, J.F. (1995). *Childhood anxiety disorders in adult panic patients.* Paper presented at the 15th annual meeting of the Anxiety Disorders Association, Pittsburgh, PA.

Pollack, M.H., Otto, M.W., Tesar, G.E., Cohen, L.S., Meltzer-Brody, S., & Rosenbaum, J.F. (1993). Long-term outcome after acute treatment with alprazolam or clonazepam for panic disorder. *Journal of Clinical Psychopharmacology, 13,* 257-263.

Pollack, M.H., & Rosenbaum, J.F. (1988). Benzodiazepines in panic-related disorders. *Journal of Anxiety Disorders, 2,* 95-107.

Pollack, M.H., Rosenbaum, J.F., Tesar, G.E., Herman, J.B., & Sachs, G.S. (1987). Clonazepam in the treatment of panic disorder and agoraphobia. *Psychopharmacology Bulletin, 23,* 141-144.

Rapee, R.M. (1995). Psychological factors influencing the affective response to biological challenge procedures in panic disorder. *Journal of Anxiety Disorders, 9,* 59-74.

Raskin, M., Peeke, H.V.S., Dickman, W., & Pinsker, H. (1982). Panic and generalized anxiety disorders: Developmental antecedents and precipitants. *Archives of General Psychiatry, 39,* 687-689.

Redmond, D.E., Huang, Y.H., Snyder, D.R., & Maas, J.W. (1976). Behavioral effects of stimulation of the nucleus locus coeruleus in the stump-tailed monkey *Macaca arctoides. Brain Research, 116,* 502-510.

Reiman, E.M., Raichle, M.E., Butler, F.K., Herscovitch, P., & Robins, E. (1984). A focal brain abnormality in panic disorder, a severe form of anxiety. *Nature, 310*(5979), 683-685.

Reiman, E.M., Raichle, M.E., Robins, E., Butler, F.K., Herscovitch, P., Fox, P., & Perlmutter, J. (1986). The application of positron emission tomography to the study of panic disorder. *American Journal of Psychiatry, 143,* 469-477.

Reiter, S.R., Otto, M.W., Pollack, M.H., & Rosenbaum, J.F. (1991). Major depression in panic disorder patients with comorbid social phobia. *Journal of Affective Disorders, 22,* 171-177.

Rickels, K., Schweizer, E., Weiss, S., & Zavodnick, S. (1993). Maintenance drug treatment for panic disorder: II. Short- and long-term outcome after drug taper. *Archives of General Psychiatry, 50,* 61-68.

Rosenbaum, J.F. (1990). A psychopharmacologist's perspective on panic disorder. *Bulletin of Menninger Clinic, 54,* 184-198.

Rosenbaum, J.F., Biederman, J., Bolduc, E.A., Hirshfeld, D.R., Faraone, S.V., & Kagan, J. (1992). Comorbidity of parental anxiety disorders as risk for childhood-onset anxiety in inhibited children. *American Journal of Psychiatry, 149,* 475-481.

Rosenbaum, J.F., Biederman, J., Gersten, M., Hirshfeld, D.R., Meminger, S.R., Herman, J.B., Kagan, J., Reznick, J.S., & Snidman, N. (1988). Behavioral inhibition in children of parents with panic disorder and agoraphobia: A controlled study. *Archives of General Psychiatry, 45,* 463-470.

Rosenbaum, J.F., Biederman, J., Hirshfeld, D.R., Bolduc, E.A., & Chaloff, J. (1991). Behavioral inhibition in children: A possible precursor to panic disorder or social phobia. *Journal of Clinical Psychiatry, 51*(11, Suppl. 5), 5-9.

Rosenbaum, J.F., Biederman, J., Hirshfeld, D.R., Bolduc, E.A., Faraone, S.V., Kagan, J., Snidman, N., & Reznick, J.S. (1991). Further evidence of an association between behavioral inhibition and anxiety disorders: Results from a family study of children from a non-clinical sample. *Journal of Psychiatry Research, 25,* 49-65.

Rosenbaum, J.F., & Gelenberg, A.J. (1991). Anxiety. In E. Bassuk, S. Schoonover, & A. Gelenberg (Eds.), *The practitioner's guide to psychoactive drugs* (3rd ed., pp. 197-218). New York: Plenum.

Roy-Byrne, P.P., Dager, S.R., Cowley, D.S., Vitaliano, P., & Dunner, D.L. (1989). Relapse and rebound following discontinuation of benzodiazepine treatment of panic attacks: Alprazolam versus diazepam. *American Journal of Psychiatry, 146,* 860-865.

Roy-Byrne, P.P., Uhde, T.W., & Post, R.M. (1986). Effect of one night's sleep deprivation on mood and behavior in panic disorder: Patients with panic disorder compared with depressed patients and normal controls. *Archives of General Psychiatry, 43,* 895-899.

Schneier, F.R., Liebowitz, M.R., Davies, S.O., Fairbanks, J., Hollander, E., Campeas, R., & Klein, D.F. (1990). Fluoxetine in panic disorder. *Journal of Clinical Psychopharmacology, 10,* 119-121.

Sheehan, D.V. (1982). Current concepts in psychiatry: Panic attacks and phobias. *New England Journal of Medicine, 307,* 156-158.

Sheehan, D.V., Ballenger, J., & Jacobsen, G. (1980). Treatment of endogenous anxiety with phobic, hysterical, and hypochondriacal symptoms. *Archives of General Psychiatry, 37,* 51-59.

Spiegel, D.A., Bruce, T.J., Gregg, S.F., & Nuzzarello, A. (1994). Does cognitive behavior therapy assist slow-taper alprazolam discontinuation in panic disorder? *American Journal of Psychiatry, 151,* 876-881.

Starcevic, V., Uhlenhuth, E.H., Kellner, R., & Pathak, D. (1992). Patterns of comorbidity in panic disorder and agoraphobia. *Psychiatry Research, 42,* 171-183.

Suomi, S.J. (1986). Anxiety-like disorders in young nonhuman primates. In R. Gittelman (Ed.), *Anxiety disorders of childhood* (pp. 1-23). New York: Guilford.

Suomi, S.J., Kraemer, G.W., Baysinger, C. M., & DeLizio, R.D. (1981). Inherited and experiential factors associated with individual differences in anxious behavior displayed by Rhesus monkeys. In D.F. Klein & J.G. Rabkin (Eds.), *Anxiety: New research and changing concepts* (pp. 179-200). New York: Raven.

Telch, M.J., Agras, S., Taylor, C.B., Roth, W.T., & Gallen, C. (1985). Combined pharmacological and behavioral treatment for agoraphobia. *Behaviour Research and Therapy, 23,* 325-335.

Telch, M.J., & Harrington, P.J. (1992, November). *Anxiety sensitivity and expectedness of arousal in mediating affective response to 35% carbon dioxide inhalation.* Paper presented at the 26th annual convention of the Association for Advancement of Behavior Therapy, Boston, MA.

Tesar, G.E., & Rosenbaum, J.F. (1993). Recognition and management of panic disorder. *Advances in Internal Medicine, 38,* 123-149.

Tesar, G.E., Rosenbaum, J.F., Pollack, M.H., Otto, M.W., Sachs, G.S., Herman, J.B., Cohen, L.S., & Spier, S.A. (1991). Double-blind, placebo-controlled comparison of clonazepam and alprazolam for panic disorder. *Journal of Clinical Psychiatry, 52,* 69-76.

Torgersen, S. (1983). Genetic factors in anxiety disorders. *Archives of General Psychiatry, 40,* 1085-1089.

Uhde, T.W. (1990). Caffeine provocation of panic: A focus on biological mechanisms. In J. Ballenger (Ed.), *Neurobiology of panic disorder* (pp. 219-242). New York: Wiley-Liss.

Uhde, T.W., Stein, M.B., Vittone, B.J., Siever, L.J., Boulenger, J.-P., Klein, E., & Mellman, T.A. (1989). Behavioral and physiologic effects of short-term and long-term administration of clonidine in panic disorder. *Archives of General Psychiatry, 46,* 170-177.

Van Vliet, I.M., Westenberg, H.G., & Den-Boer, J.A. (1993). MAO inhibitors in panic disorder: Clinical effects of treatment with brofaromine: A double blind placebo controlled study. *Psychopharmacology, 112,* 483-489.

Versiani, M., Nardi, A.E., Mundim, F.D., Alves, A.B., Liebowitz, M.R., & Amrein, R. (1992). Pharmacotherapy of social phobia: A controlled study with moclobemide and phenelzine. *British Journal of Psychiatry, 161,* 353-360.

Weissman, M.M., & Merikangas, K.R. (1986). The epidemiology of anxiety and panic disorders: An update. *Journal of Clinical Psychiatry, 47*(6, Suppl.), 11-17.

Woods, S.W., & Charney, D.S. (1988). Applications of the pharmacologic challenge strategy in panic disorders research. *Journal of Anxiety Disorders, 2,* 31-49.

Woods, S.W., Charney, D.S., Goodman, W.K., & Heninger, G.R. (1988). Carbon dioxide-induced anxiety: Behavioral, physiologic, and biochemical effects of carbon dioxide in patients with panic disorders and healthy subjects. *Archives of General Psychiatry, 45,* 43-52.

Zitrin, C.M., & Ross, D.C. (1988). Early separation anxiety and adult agoraphobia. *Journal of Nervous and Mental Disease, 176,* 621-625.

2. Integrated Treatment of Social Phobia

John R. Marshall, MD

Substantial progress has been made in the understanding and treatment of social phobia. Since its identification and delineation from other disorders in 1980 in *DSM-III,* professional levels of recognition have substantially risen. However, understanding and awareness for the general public have not followed suit. Most patients we see have not sought help for their social anxiety, or it has been lost among other symptoms, not identified or complained of to someone who could provide treatment.

We have begun to realize that social phobia is much more prevalent than originally believed. Initial studies suggested a lifetime prevalence of 1.8-3.2% (Regier et al., 1988), but more recent surveys with improved diagnostic methods suggest a 7.9% one-year prevalence and a lifetime prevalence as high as 13.3% (Kessler et al., 1994). If accurate, these findings mean that social phobia is the second most common mental disorder in the United States.

We are now able to describe other characteristics of this disorder as it affects the general population. Social phobia has a female-to-male ratio of approximately 2.5 to 1, its mean age of onset is early (11-15 years), and onset after age 25 is uncommon (Burke, Burke, Regier, & Rae, 1990; Schneier, Johnson, Hornig, Liebowitz, & Weissman, 1992). The fact that social phobia tends to strike at a critical time of life (i.e., adolescence and young adulthood) may explain the surprisingly high rate of disability and the unrelenting chronicity of this disorder. We know that social phobia patients can be disabled in virtually all areas of life. Common sequelae are failure to complete school and abandonment of higher education goals. More than 70% of persons with social phobia are in the lowest two quartiles of socioeconomic status; in one study, 22.3% of patients with pure social phobia were currently on welfare (Schneier et al., 1992). We also know there is a dramatic effect on one's human relationships. More than half of those with social phobia are single, divorced, or separated. Suicide attempts may be 15.7% higher than in the general population (Schneier et al., 1992).

Research promising to tease apart the etiological components of social phobia is continuing. One promising area is the search to characterize the neurobiology. Progress has been made in delineating social

---

Dr. Marshall is the director of The Anxiety Disorders Center at the University of Wisconsin Hospital and Clinics, Madison, Wisconsin.

phobia from certain other disorders, especially panic disorder. We also know certain physiological and hormonal systems that do not appear to be affected, such as the hypothalamic-pituitary-adrenal axis and the hypothalamic-pituitary-thyroid axis, but we are less sure about where abnormalities may occur (Tancer, 1993). Preliminary studies suggest possible dysregulation in both dopaminergic and serotonergic systems (Davidson et al., 1993). Tancer (1993) suggested the existence of postsynaptic receptor supersensitivity. Newly developed technologies, such as magnetic resonance imaging and magnetic resonance spectroscopy, are being brought to bear, but at this time findings remain nonspecific (Davidson et al., 1993; Potts, Davidson, & Krishnan, 1993).

Progress has also been made in establishing broader models of etiology. Original studies of inhibited children by Kagan, Reznick, and Snidman (1988), expanded by Rosenbaum, Biederman, Pollack, and Hirshfeld (1994) to include parents, suggest a diathesis of anxiety proneness, possibly representing an inherited physiological predisposition to the development of severe social anxiety. The ultimate manifestation of this proneness might then depend on the extent of the dysregulation or on the interaction of this predisposition with environmental factors, including parental psychopathology (Rosenbaum et al., 1994).

The pharmacological treatment of social phobia

There is little question that social phobia, disabling as it is, deserves aggressive treatment. Although clinical practitioners seem to be giving more consideration to psychopharmacological interventions, the usual reasons for not using medication still prevail: failing to recognize the disorder, considering it a condition that responds only to behavioral interventions, and viewing it as substantially a personality trait and therefore not responsive to medication. Most of the social phobia patients in our anxiety clinic have not been previously treated or appropriately treated, and often they are seeking treatment after years of suffering severe symptoms. Advances in the use of pharmacological agents are not so much about recently developed new agents, but rather are about more careful selection of the particularly appropriate drug, as well as increased appreciation of the substantial comorbidity associated with social phobia. The selection of a medication efficacious for both (or all) disorders can be critical to successful amelioration of symptoms with fewer agents and/or side effects.

Beta-adrenergic blockers
The clinical use of beta-adrenergic blockers for social phobia appears

to have been stimulated by psychological theories suggesting that anxiety is at least in part a response to perceived somatic sensations. These specific symptoms include dry mouth, palpitations, sweating, blushing, and tremor (i.e., hyperactivity of the beta-adrenergic nervous system). Clinical use was also reinforced by the observation that for years, professional performers, including singers and instrumentalists, have been relying substantially on beta blockers to overcome stage fright (performance anxiety) (Fishbein & Middlestadt, 1987/1988). This use has been largely without medical supervision, and the performers strongly believe that the drugs are effective.

Indeed, controlled studies of actual performance, including blind ratings, have shown beneficial effects on various types of performance (Brantigan, Brantigan, & Joseph, 1982). Initial open studies of social phobia with these drugs suggested clinical usefulness; however, in a larger, well-controlled study, beta blockers were found to be ineffective for generalized forms of social phobia (Liebowitz, Fyer, Gorman, Campeas, & Levin, 1986; Liebowitz, Gorman, Fyer, & Kline, 1985). This study confirms our own experience, which suggests that beta blockers are most effective when the required performance situation is circumscribed and when patients have generally low social anxiety in other situations.

The positive effects of beta blockers appear related to the suppression of autonomic cues, but the lack of effectiveness for generalized social phobia likely occurs because cognitive anxiety levels are only indirectly and modestly altered. Studies have shown that persons with specific social phobia demonstrate higher heart rates in performance situations than do those with generalized social phobia (Heimberg, Hope, Dodge, & Becker, 1990). The drugs most commonly used in these situations include propranolol and atenolol. The latter may be preferable because there appears to be less likelihood of adverse central nervous system side effects, and the effective action of the drug is longer.

Monoamine oxidase inhibitors

The monoamine oxidase inhibitors (MAOIs) appear to have the greatest efficacy in the treatment of social phobia, although there are few direct comparison studies. Liebowitz et al. (1985) first suggested the use of this class of drugs, in part because of their experiences with atypical depressive patients who demonstrated excessive interpersonal sensitivity, a characteristic of social phobia patients. Their initial open trial and subsequent controlled trials documented the efficacy of phenelzine (Gelernter et al., 1991; Liebowitz et al., 1986; Liebowitz et al., 1992). Other studies showed tranylcypromine to be similarly effective (Versiani, Mundim, Nardi, & Liebowitz, 1988). This class of drugs is often avoided by practitioners because of common side effects and the possibility of a hypertensive crisis that necessitates a low tyramine diet. Two new MAOIs, moclobemide and brofaromine, appear to have the advantages of fewer side effects, a lowered risk of hypertensive crisis, and consequently less need for dietary restriction. Although presently marketed in Europe for depression, they are not available in the United States, and it does not appear that they will be in the near future.

MAOIs may be the first drug to consider for several commonly found comorbid conditions. Substantial numbers of social phobia patients also suffer from panic disorder (Rosenbaum & Pollack, 1994). Some studies place this comorbidity rate as high as 48% (Starcevic, Uhlenhuth, Kellner, & Pathak, 1992). Panic disorder, both with and without agoraphobia, has been shown to respond to MAOIs. Carrasco, Hollander, Schneier, and Liebowitz (1992) have also observed that another anxiety disorder, obsessive-compulsive disorder, when present with social phobia, may be preferentially treated with MAOIs. Although generalized anxiety disorder is commonly found with social phobia, studies on the effectiveness of MAOIs for this disorder are lacking at this time. The MAOIs are, of course, antidepressants and are therefore a likely choice when comorbid depression is present. Given the dietary restrictions necessary with MAOIs and the high levels of side effects, most clinicians prefer a trial of selective serotonin reuptake inhibitors (SSRIs) as a first-line treatment (perhaps in association with a benzodiazepine). With atypical depression, beginning with a MAOI might be preferable (tricyclics have not proven effective for social phobia). At least one case study reported the successful treatment of social phobia and avoidant personality disorder with MAOIs (Deltito & Perugi, 1986). We continue to debate where to draw the line between social phobia and avoidant personality disorder. Our positive experiences in this area reflect the need to not "write off" persons with personality disorder diagnoses, particularly avoidant personality, as being nonresponsive to pharmacological interventions.

Selective serotonin reuptake inhibitors

There are now five open trials describing the potential usefulness of selective serotonin reuptake inhibitors (SSRIs) in the treatment of social phobia (Davidson, 1994). These reports seem to indicate moderately positive results using fluoxetine. It should be kept in mind that direct comparisons of effectiveness with other classes of medications, as well as with other SSRIs, are lacking. Successful treatment of social phobia with other SSRIs has not been reported. As noted, although the SSRIs, in our experience, appear slightly less effective for the treatment of core social phobia, this class of drugs might be a first-line treatment for comorbid depression to possibly provide treatment without additional agents. If needed, benzodiazepines can be safely used with SSRIs.

Social phobia is the anxiety disorder with the highest comorbid alcohol abuse. This finding suggests the SSRIs as a first choice in the presence of a past history of drug or alcohol abuse or when there is a questionable state of ongoing abuse.

It is also important to note several other conditions that have a high incidence of comorbidity with social phobia. They include eating disorders, both bulimia and anorexia; there is evidence that the SSRIs are useful in the treatment of these conditions (Brewerton, Lydiard, Ballenger, & Herzog, 1993; Halmi et al., 1991). Less commonly, body dysmorphic disorder and certain paraphilias are disorders for which there has been some speculation about the role of social phobia (Golwyn & Sevlie, 1992). Both these conditions have occasionally been successfully treated with SSRIs. An interesting and useful side effect of the SSRIs in socially anxious young males is the inhibition of premature ejaculation by this class of medications.

Benzodiazepines
The benzodiazepines have been a valuable addition to the treatment of social phobia. Their implementation for this use is a natural follow-up to their recognized effectiveness in the treatment of other anxiety disorders. There have been five open trials and two controlled studies. Davidson's (1994) study of clonazepam was the largest, with substantial improvement occurring rapidly and with maximal improvement at 8 weeks. The mean dosage was 2.1 mg per day.

The effectiveness of the high-potency benzodiazepines in panic disorder suggests their suitability as the treatment of choice for the common co-occurrence of panic disorder and social phobia. For comorbid depression, a combination of either the SSRIs or the MAOIs with a benzodiazepine can be used. The well-known high incidence of alcohol abuse among social phobia patients warrants careful investigation of patients' drinking patterns prior to the use of benzodiazepines. In my view, however, the absolute contraindication of this class of drugs is unwarranted, particularly if the patient has abstained from alcohol for a substantial period (Marshall, 1994a). There are patients for whom the SSRIs and MAOIs are not effective or for some reason are not tolerated. We need to remind ourselves that the benzodiazepines, compared to many other agents often used for anxiety, are not as highly addictive as commonly believed. One needs to weigh the potential "theoretical" impact of the benzodiazepine on the drinking behavior versus the overall morbidity and disability associated with the combined condition. Also, the common onset of social phobia before alcohol abuse, as well as patients' descriptions of their drinking behavior, suggests a strong "self-medication" pattern. Frequently, if the anxiety is adequately treated, this pattern can be interrupted and alcohol consumption can be reduced or abstained from.

A side effect not commonly mentioned in the literature but occasionally seen in anxiety clinics is the disinhibition of social behavior associated with higher doses of clonazepam. The situation may come to one's attention via complaints of the spouse, who perhaps notes that the patient appears irritable, "talks back," "tells people off easily," or is unduly assertive. Sometimes it is difficult to sort out appropriate social behavior, which is so markedly different from the patient's usual baseline behavior that it is believed to be pathological. Usually a simple lowering of the dose, discussions, and education of the concerned individuals ameliorate this problem.

Other medications
Several other medications have been identified as potentially useful in the treatment of social phobia. In two open trials, buspirone has shown some success in ameliorating symptoms (Clark & Agras, 1991; Schneier et al., 1993). A few patients were described as having rather significant responses, but most improvement was modest. One case report describes clonidine as being successful in the treatment of blushing (Goldstein, 1987), and another reports success with bupropion (Emmanuel, Lydiard, & Ballenger, 1991).

Psychotherapeutic interventions

There are many reasons to include appropriate psychotherapeutic interventions as part of the integrated treatment of social phobia. Some patients prefer not to use medications, others are unable to tolerate them for various reasons, and certain highly specific social phobias lend themselves primarily to behavioral interventions (e.g., difficulty urinating in public rest rooms). We also do not know how long medication should be used, and relapse rates are high when patients are treated only with medication. In our clinic, for moderate to severely distressed social phobia patients, we recommend psychotherapy in conjunction with drug treatment. It should be noted, however, that thus far there are no studies to support the intuitively attractive notion that both modalities are superior to either alone. Recent studies suggest that for some patients treated with certain highly specific psychotherapies, the two approaches may be comparable (Heimberg & Juster, 1994).

The lead in the psychotherapies of social phobia has clearly been taken by those with cognitive and/or behavioral interests. Techniques that have been studied include social skills training, in vivo exposure, applied relaxation, and various "packages" that have integrated cognitive and behavioral components (Heimberg & Barlow, 1991). Supporters of cognitive-behavioral therapy (CBT) argue that it contributes to long-term maintenance of gains. There are few studies of other psychotherapeutic modalities applied to social phobia, and I know of no studies specifically using psychodynamic interventions.

CBT is based on the belief that certain cognitions play a role in the development and maintenance of social fears and phobias. Described by multiple investigators, these approaches emphasize the negative cognitions experienced in anticipation of, or during, social situations; the expectation of negative consequences as a result of actual or feared behaviors; and overall cognitive biases regarding information with an evaluative component (Heimberg, 1993).

We have observed that the confrontation and eventual alteration of these beliefs and behaviors occurs most effectively in a group setting. Using concepts borrowed substantially from treatments described by the Albany Social Phobia Program, our therapy groups meet for 12 weekly sessions of 1½ hours each; groups are composed exclusively of social phobia patients (Heimberg & Juster, 1994). Although groups are time-limited, participants may repeat the group series and often do so. Components of the therapy sessions include substantial education about social phobia with a cognitive-behavioral orientation, the production and subsequent identification of specific cognitions that commonly occur in response to socially threatening situations, and exposure to the anxiety-provoking situations in the context of group interactions. Initially, the leaders and eventually the group members identify the reoccurring negative cognitions that are produced in connection with ongoing group exercises. Homework assignments are commonly used, and patients subsequently report their experiences and suggestions for alterations in both behavior and thought patterns.

The elements of successful therapy

Of course, most of us are not formally trained in cognitive-behavioral techniques, and practical referral sources may not be available. Unless one specializes in treating anxiety disorders, the practitioner may not have sufficient numbers of social phobia patients to establish groups. Some key elements and strategies, however, can be extrapolated from more formal programs. Social phobia patients, like other anxiety patients, have an underlying fear of loss of control. They are often ashamed of their symptoms, have never talked about them, and are convinced that their own fears are strange and unique. Education plays a major role in demystifying the condition, helping patients to see that it is a defined disorder that can be understood and treated, and that substantial numbers of other persons suffer from the same symptoms. Patients are also helped by understanding that everyone responds to being scrutinized or to performing with some degree of anxiety or arousal, as well as with similar symptoms. In addition to explanations in therapy sessions, we suggest readings. *Social Phobia* (Marshall, 1994b) is recommended for an overview of the disorder, and other books with more specific self-help advice are also suggested (e.g., Markway, 1992).

A second major element that should continually be emphasized is the importance of exposure and the associated phenomena of desensitization. Particularly when beginning a medication, patients often report that its efficacy is minimal or absent. However, in subsequent examinations of their behavior, it becomes apparent that they have not exposed themselves to the feared situations. Once encouraged to do so, patients sometimes report—often with amazement—a dramatic diminishment of anxiety or significant social successes of which they had been unaware.

Other patients may insist they do not avoid feared social situations, or that they are exposing themselves to such situations. However, careful exploration in the therapy sessions reveals that they are employing mechanisms to lessen the impact of the situation. Common techniques include distraction ("being somewhere else in my mind"), avoiding true participation in group settings, and generally keeping a "low profile" (e.g., speaking only with persons considered "safe," avoiding other feared aspects of the situation). Careful review highlights these avoidant maneuvers. Mutual agreement on homework assignments and encouragement to maintain repetitive practice are cornerstones of therapy, even if patients are not receiving formal behavior therapy.

The continued focus in therapy sessions on specific encounters and responses leads naturally to the important element of identifying and discussing flawed cognitions. Gentle challenge, humor, mock exaggeration of consequences, and reinforcement of alternative interpretations are integral to the psychotherapy of social phobia. The therapist plays the role of a supportive coach dissecting, restructuring, and working through feared situations while encouraging and reassuring the patient.

Finally—but not least—a crucial element to successful treatment is the therapeutic relationship. Common descriptions of behavioral approaches tend to portray the therapist as a technician or mechanic, fixing something that is broken. As many have emphasized, change occurs best in the context of a therapeutic relationship in which there is trust and a subsequent feeling of safety. This relationship is especially important for anxiety patients, most of whom are fearful, and for social phobia patients, who may also suffer from poor or few relationships. A psychodynamic contribution to treatment can be useful in the examination of adverse countertransference ideas, such as, "I'm anxious, too, in social situations, but I got over it," which minimizes the patient's distress (Zerbe, 1994). The active therapeutic stance does not obviate the need to listen. Recurring common themes are perturbations in relationships as persons with social phobia grow and expand their horizons; guilt, shame, and grief for what could have been; and the restructuring of the self-image as repeated successes occur. Patients may feel disloyal to others as they begin to ask for more for themselves in life. Those of us originally trained in psychodynamic therapy should be ideally equipped for hearing and understanding those issues that arise as a result of more specific therapeutic interventions. Effective therapy for social phobia requires a thoughtful integration of multiple therapeutic frameworks.

References

Brantigan, C.O., Brantigan, T.A., & Joseph, N. (1982). Effect of beta blockade and beta stimulation on stage fright. *American Journal of Medicine, 72,* 88-94.

Brewerton, T.D., Lydiard, R.B., Ballenger, J.C., & Herzog, D.B. (1993). Eating disorders and social phobia. *Archives of General Psychiatry, 50,* 70.

Burke, K.C., Burke, J.D., Regier, D.A., & Rae, D.S. (1990). Age at onset of selected mental disorders in five community populations. *Archives of General Psychiatry, 47,* 511-518.

Carrasco, J.L., Hollander, E., Schneier, F.R., & Liebowitz, M.R. (1992). Treatment outcome of obsessive compulsive disorder with comorbid social phobia. *Journal of Clinical Psychiatry, 53,* 387-391.

Clark, D.B., & Agras, W.S. (1991). The assessment and treatment of performance anxiety in musicians. *American Journal of Psychiatry, 148,* 598-605.

Davidson, J.R.T. (1994). Social phobia: Outlook for the '90s. *Journal of Clinical Psychiatry, 55,* 503-510.

Davidson, J.R.T., Krishnan, K.R.R., Charles, H.C., Boyko, O., Potts, N.L.S., Ford, S.M., & Patterson, L. (1993). Magnetic resonance spectroscopy in social phobia: Preliminary findings. *Journal of Clinical Psychiatry, 54*(12, Suppl.), 19-25.

Deltito, J.A., & Perugi, G. (1986). A case of social phobia with avoidant personality disorder treated with MAOI. *Comprehensive Psychiatry, 27,* 255-258.

Emmanuel, N.P., Lydiard, R.B., & Ballenger, J.C. (1991). Treatment of social phobia with bupropion. *Journal of Clinical Psychopharmacology, 11,* 276-277.

Fishbein, M., & Middlestadt, S.E. (with Ottati, V., Strauss, S., & Ellis, A.). (1988). Medical problems among ICSOM musicians: Overview of a national survey. *Medical Problems of Performing Artists, 3*(1), 1-8. (Original work published 1987)

Gelernter, C.S., Uhde, T.W., Cimbolic, P., Arnkof, D.B., Vittone, B.J., Tancer, M.E., & Bartko, J.J. (1991). Cognitive-behavioral and pharmacologic treatments of social phobia: A controlled study. *Archives of General Psychiatry, 48,* 938-945.

Goldstein, S. (1987). Treatment of social phobia with clonidine. *Biological Psychiatry, 22,* 369-372.

Golwyn, D.H., & Sevlie, C.P. (1992). Paraphilias, nonparaphilic sexual addictions, and social phobia. *Journal of Clinical Psychiatry, 53,* 330.

Halmi, K.A., Eckert, E., Marchi, P., Sampugnaro, V., Apple, R., & Cohen, J. (1991). Comorbidity of psychiatric diagnosis in anorexia nervosa. *Archives of General Psychiatry, 48,* 712-718.

Heimberg, R.G. (1993). Specific issues in the cognitive-behavioral treatment of social phobia. *Journal of Clinical Psychiatry, 54,* 36-45.

Heimberg, R.G., & Barlow, D.H. (1991). New developments in cognitive-behavioral therapy for social phobia. *Journal of Clinical Psychiatry, 52*(11, Suppl.), 21-30.

Heimberg, R.G., Hope, D.A., Dodge, C.S., & Becker, R.E. (1990). DSM-III-R subtypes of social phobia: Comparison of generalized social phobics and public speaking phobics. *Journal of Nervous and Mental Disease, 178,* 172-179.

Heimberg, R.G., & Juster, H.R. (1994). Treatment of social phobia in cognitive-behavioral groups. *Journal of Clinical Psychiatry, 55*(6, Suppl.), 38-46.

Kagan, J., Reznick, J.S., & Snidman, N. (1988). Temperamental influences on reactions to unfamiliarity and challenge. *Advances in Experimental Medical Biology, 245,* 319-339.

Kessler, R.C., McGonagle, K.A., Zhao, S., Nelson, C.B., Hughes, M., Eshleman, S., Wittchen, H.-U., & Kendler, K.S. (1994). Lifetime and 12-month prevalence of DSM-III-R psychiatric disorders in the United States: Results from the National Comorbidity Survey. *Archives of General Psychiatry, 51,* 8-19.

Liebowitz, M.R., Fyer, A.J., Gorman, J.M., Campeas, R., & Levin, A. (1986). Phenelzine in social phobia. *Journal of Clinical Psychopharmacology, 6,* 93-98.

Liebowitz, M.R., Gorman, J.M., Fyer, A.J., & Kline, D.F. (1985). Social phobia: Review of a neglected anxiety disorder. *Archives of General Psychiatry, 42,* 729-736.

Liebowitz, M.R., Schneier, F.R., Campeas, R., Hollander, E., Hatterer, J., Fyer, A., Gorman, J., Papp, L., Davis, S., Gully, R., & Klein, D.F. (1992). Phenelzine vs. atenolol in social phobia: A placebo-controlled comparison. *Archives of General Psychiatry, 49,* 290-300.

Markway, B. (1992). *Dying of embarrassment: Help for social anxiety and social phobia.* Oakland, CA: New Harbinger.

Marshall, J.R. (1994a). The diagnosis and treatment of social phobia and alcohol abuse. *Bulletin of the Menninger Clinic, 58*(2, Suppl. A), A58-A66.

Marshall, J.R. (1994b). *Social phobia: From shyness to stage fright.* New York: BasicBooks.

Potts, N.L.S., Davidson, J.R.T., & Krishnan, K.R.R. (1993). The role of nuclear magnetic resonance imaging in psychiatric research. *Journal of Clinical Psychiatry, 54*(12, Suppl.), 13-18.

Regier, D.A., Boyd, J.H., Burke, J.D., Rae, D.S., Myers, J.K., Kramer, M., Robins, L.N., George, L.K., Karno, M., & Locke, B.Z. (1988). One-month prevalence of mental disorders in the United States: Based on five Epidemiological Catchment Area sites. *Archives of General Psychiatry, 45,* 977-986.

Rosenbaum, J.F., Biederman, J., Pollack, R.A., & Hirshfeld, D.R. (1994). The etiology of social phobia. *Journal of Clinical Psychiatry, 55*(6, Suppl.), 10-16.

Rosenbaum, J.F., & Pollack, R.A. (1994). The psychopharmacology of social phobia and comorbid disorders. *Bulletin of the Menninger Clinic, 58*(2, Suppl. A), A67-A83.

Schneier, F.R., Johnson, J., Hornig, C.D., Liebowitz, M.R., & Weissman, M.M. (1992). Social phobia: Comorbidity and morbidity in an epidemiologic sample. *Archives of General Psychiatry, 49,* 282-288.

Schneier, F.R., Saoud, J.B., Campeas, R., Fallon, B.A., Hollander, E., Coplan, J., & Liebowitz, M.R. (1993). Buspirone in social phobia. *Journal of Clinical Psychopharmacology, 13,* 251-256.

Starcevic, V., Uhlenhuth, E.H., Kellner, R., & Pathak, D. (1992). Patterns of comorbidity in panic disorder and agoraphobia. *Psychiatry Research, 42,* 171-183.

Tancer, M.E. (1993). Neurobiology of social phobia. *Journal of Clinical Psychiatry, 54*(12, Suppl.), 26-30.

Versiani, M., Mundim, F.D., & Nardi, A.E., & Liebowitz, M.R. (1988). Tranylcypromine in social phobia. *Journal of Clinical Psychopharmacology, 8,* 279-283.

Zerbe, K.J. (1994). Uncharted waters: Psychodynamic considerations in the diagnosis and treatment of social phobia. *Bulletin of the Menninger Clinic, 58*(2, Suppl. A), A3-A20.

3. Anxiety Disorders in Women

Kathryn J. Zerbe, MD

A young woman furtively glances at her watch. It seems as though she has been waiting for hours for her appointment when only moments have passed. She scans the hallway that leads to the doctor's office door while she scratches the nape of her neck with a brittle fingernail, jagged and stubby from nervous nibbles. Even as she tries to divert her thoughts to other matters, she is noticeably preoccupied with the consequences of the upcoming interview. Growing more queasy and pale by the moment, she frets that she will flounder at even the simplest questions and that her budding career will be stymied.

The plight of this interviewee is not unique. Indeed, most clinicians of either gender will easily identify with the predicament of the young, insecure student who anticipates at least subtle censure on the part of the distinguished senior physician who will interview her. As she attempts to minimize the physiological concomitants of anxiety by falsely appearing self-assured, calm, and in control, her subtle psychomotor shifts and twitches betray her; low self-esteem and imminent sense of failure become manifest by the jumpiness, fearfulness, and tremulousness she experiences when the interviewer invites her into his office.

This familiar vignette raises many questions about the diagnosis, understanding, and treatment of anxiety disorders in women. For example, is the interviewee manifesting symptoms of a bona fide anxiety disorder, or is she exhibiting a situational problem that will abate once the stress is over? Has the individual been struggling with these symptoms in other areas of her life; if so, for how long? Does a medical condition complicate her presentation or even predispose to it? Are her difficulties the only manifestation of her anxiety or, on looking more deeply, will we find more dramatic manifestations of illness? Specifically, does she also suffer from vivid obsessions and relentless compulsions? Does her timidity reach such proportions that her forays into social situations are compromised (e.g., social phobia)? Have there been any paroxysms of anxiety so intense as to warrant a diagnosis of panic attack? Does she have biological relatives afflicted with similar difficulties? Perhaps she also suffers from other psychiatric problems (e.g., comorbidity). Finally, what role do social and cultural factors play in exacerbating this woman's fears

---

Dr. Zerbe is vice president for Education and Research at The Menninger Clinic, Topeka, Kansas.

about her gender and career roles? Is she more prone to an anxiety attack than her male peers because she is a woman entering a profession or career closed to past generations of females?

The pioneering spirit, although publicly lauded and romantically heralded, is fraught with pain and insecurity. Contemporary women may be predisposed to the symptoms of anxiety—if not full-blown anxiety disorders—because we tread new paths without the benefit of seasoned mentors or the same organizational supports as men, and without sustained affirmation from the family and larger social network. When addressing the problem of anxiety disorders in women, one must realize that gender-based research is in its infancy. Thus the subject is one where there is likely to be rapid evolution and reevaluation of many of the core issues discussed here. Yet this exciting area holds great promise for the future of both genders, as evaluation and treatment will truly be tailored to the specific needs of each individual man or woman.

Medical issues

In the evaluation of the anxious patient, medical conditions that present with anxiety must always be initially ruled out (Wise & Griffies, 1995). Drugs of abuse (e.g., amphetamines, cocaine), caffeine, and alcohol may all precipitate anxiety attacks in women. In addition, medical illnesses may engender particular stressors that lead to uneasiness, worry, and even panic.

Although an array of medical etiologies may predispose to anxiety, some disorders in particular must be carefully considered in the female population. Coronary conditions such as angina pectoris, dysrhythmias, valvular disease—especially mitral valve prolapse—and congestive heart failure are frequently accompanied by dread and apprehension. Because coronary disease in women has been underappreciated (Clark, Janz, Dodge, & Garrity, 1994; Judelson, 1994; Wenger, 1994), sensitivity to gender-related issues will help the clinician to more accurately assess cardiac symptomatology and the acute anxiety that often accompanies it in women.

Other medical causes of anxiety that particularly affect women are hyperthyroidism, systemic lupus erythematosus, and anemia. Although overall smoking rates have declined since 1974, teenage women have the highest increase in smoking rates. Smoking predisposes them to respiratory conditions such as asthma, chronic obstructive pulmonary disease, and pneumonia. Each of these respiratory conditions may also be etiological for anxiety symptoms and must be ruled out.

It is imperative that the physician take a thorough history, including noting *all* prescribed and over-the-counter medications. Those women who use nonsteroidal anti-inflammatory agents, steroids, psychostimulants for dieting, or pseudoephedrine compounds for allergies or upper respiratory infections may present with a subthreshold or full-blown anxiety attack because of medication side effects. The list of drugs known to precipitate anxiety is long, and full discussion of medication side effects is beyond the scope of this paper. It is essential, however, for the therapist to be vigilant with respect to all the medical contributors that may precipitate, exaggerate, or mask anxiety disorders.

Epidemiological and diagnostic perspectives

Population-based studies with respect to gender differences have thus far yielded less robust information about the anxiety disorders than about depressive syndromes. This fertile area of investigation will continue to yield important data about the boundary issues influencing the diagnosis of particular anxiety disorders in subclinical populations (Brown, Barlow, & Liebowitz, 1994; Judd, 1994) and in those with comorbid conditions. Anxiety disorders, particularly panic disorder, somatization, and generalized anxiety disorders, are psychiatric disorders also frequently observed in women with depression (Pajer, 1995). A separate category of "mixed anxiety-depression" has been proposed to encompass disorders that are now considered subthreshold with respect to current diagnostic practices and that clearly describe a substantial cohort of women whose lives are impeded by a host of affective, autonomic, and cognitive symptomatology.

Additional population-based studies on the delineated anxiety disorders, mixed anxiety-depression syndromes, and subthreshold disorders will confirm or refute the 3:1 ratio generally conceded to be the gap in the prevalence between women and men with respect to anxiety disorders. This information will also help us to integrate advances in psychiatric epidemiology by incorporating putative environmental risk factors and potential investigator biases that influence diagnostic practice with both genders.

With these caveats in mind, it is important to underscore the recent research on the role of familial and genetic factors in the etiology of the anxiety disorders. Kendler, Neale, Kessler, Heath, and Eaves (1992) examined 1,033 female twin pairs from a population-based registry. These researchers found that generalized anxiety disorder is moderately familial, tending to run in families. Although the heritability of this condition was deemed to be modest (approximately

30%), environmental experiences were found to play "a critical role in determining who will become affected" (p. 269). Sex-specific transmission could not be determined from the results, nor could they be deemed generalizable to the nontwin population.

In a later report, Kendler and colleagues (1993) argued against a view, held since the 1980s, that panic disorder in women is due to a highly penetrant single major locus on the genome. Using a multifactorial-threshold model, they reported a heritability range of 30-40%, arguing for only a modest heritability for panic disorder in the general population. After attempting to delineate whether panic disorder was due to genetic or shared familial environment, they concluded that there is great difficulty in discriminating between genetic and familial-environmental transmission. The authors themselves contrasted the low heritability of panic disorders with the estimate of more than 65% for schizophrenia and manic-depressive illness.

Although not highlighting it in their paper, Kendler et al. (1993) noted the diagnostic difficulty in assessing panic disorder in a general population and the ambiguities involved in delineating what constitutes situational and spontaneous phobic avoidance and panic in some individuals. While acknowledging the strides of the past decade in teasing out biological components and diagnostic discriminating factors of anxiety disorders (Roy-Byrne & Cowley, 1988), these studies suggest that much is yet to be mined in the field as a whole. Diagnostic verification among even the most highly trained raters remains murky. These facts are particularly cogent and humbling, because diagnosis and treatment of women have been used to stereotype or undergird their position as the "weaker vessel" (Fraser, 1984; Shorter, 1991).

Elaborating on the problem of verifiable diagnosis, reports have consistently shown that anxiety disorders are among those psychiatric syndromes with the lowest diagnostic agreement. Recent reports have sought to more thoroughly discriminate between categories and are to be encouraged so that, over the next decade, both women and men can partake of highly specific treatment modalities based on the targeting of specific symptoms. Psychiatric treatment will move forward as truly comparative outcome studies of anxiety disorders are undertaken.

Some preliminary reports based on single-case studies have shown that targeting the worry associated with generalized anxiety disorders may be highly efficacious (Brown, Barlow, & Liebowitz, 1994; Brown, O'Leary, & Barlow, 1993). One question raised by these reports is whether one gender is more responsive than the other to the targeting of particular symptoms by a specific therapeutic trial, a kind of "sex-linked intervention." However, this question, always difficult to study because of the myriad of factors it is necessary to unravel, is even more complicated in an age of political correctness. Now both men and women investigators are likely to feel upbraided by gender politics from the most conservative to the most ardent feminist camps should their findings be found antithetical to an opposing viewpoint.

Interactions between anxiety, work, and the reproductive cycle

In the psychodynamic literature, the seasons of a woman's life from menarche to menopause have been discussed and interpreted in light of anxiety's impact (Barnett & Baruch, 1978; Benedek, 1959; Horney, 1926; Kestenberg, 1976; Nadelson, 1989; Penn, 1986). As more women have entered the workplace, psychotherapists have also observed that women now present for treatment with conflicts about success and failure in their careers (Applegarth, 1986; Moulton, 1986; Nadelson, 1989). For some individuals, success engenders concern about the loss of love (Person, 1988); it may also bring to the surface underlying low self-esteem exemplified by apprehension, worry, insecurity, cognitive befuddlement, shyness and social anxiety, and ruminative concerns about gender roles and social propriety. We may thus assume that, as men's and women's roles change—confronted as we are by a more complex, fast-paced society—we will find and have to confront more anxiety in ourselves and in other persons who superficially appear to "have it all."

We may also hypothesize that earlier agrarian societies posed fewer anxiety-generating issues and concerns because they were less competitive, possessed more sustaining social bonds, and presented fewer anxiety-triggering social situations than our own. One might also argue that bona fide anxiety disorders, although present, were less apparent because individuals who suffered from them were not pushed to perform in their cultures and did not present for treatment with the same, if any, symptom patterns (Appignanesi & Forrester, 1992; Shorter, 1991).

A recent series of case reports has described phenomenologically a host of anxiety disorders related to the postpartum period. Anxiety during pregnancy, particularly the first and last trimesters, has been well described, and the high rate of depressive symptomatology in the postpartum period is well known to psychiatric, primary care, and gynecological subspecialties. These newer reports augment what has been observed about the postpartum period with respect to panic disorder, obsessive-compulsive disorder, and generalized anxiety disorder.

New mothers frequently experience a host of concerns about the care of their babies. A continuum of worries abound, ranging from the overall care and well-being of the infant to obsessional preoccupation about harm, disease, and despair about one's competency as a mother. One patient, a woman in her early 30s, presented for her second psychiatric admission after the birth of her first child. Intrusive thoughts and obsessive rituals about the baby had to be teased apart from her delusionally based thought disturbance of an earlier psychiatric illness. In a discussion of a case series of patients with postpartum onset of obsessive-compulsive illness, Sichel, Cohen, Rosenbaum, and Driscoll (1993) hypothesized that the rapid decline of estrogen and progesterone has an adverse effect on serotonergic function, leading to the acute onset of obsessive-compulsive disorder in some patients. Because their patients responded so well to treatment with serotonergic reuptake blockers, Sichel et al. speculated that an interaction between the rapidly changing reproductive hormonal milieu and a predisposition to psychiatric disorders, rather than an individual's adjustment to motherhood, may underlie obsessive-compulsive thoughts and actions in the puerperium. Sichel, Cohen, Dimmock, and Rosenbaum (1993) went on to argue that mental health professionals must educate other specialists about the presence and high morbidity of the anxiety disorders, particularly obsessive-compulsive disorder, in the postpartum period, because failure to treat this population will have profoundly negative effects on the infant, the mother, and the entire family.

The phenomenological literature remains scant with respect to the actual incidence and course of anxiety disorders during each trimester of pregnancy; more work must be done in this area to shed light on actual incidence, course of illness, and impact on mother, fetus, and family (Cohen, Heller, & Rosenbaum, 1989). When the pregnant woman presents with a bona fide anxiety disorder, obvious care must be taken to regulate her psychotropic medication. Certainly, to avoid teratogenicity, the lowest dose of medications must be used. Hence most authorities recommend tricyclic antidepressants for patients who require pharmacotherapy for a panic or other anxiety disorder because this class of drugs has a long history of use with minimal documented effects to the fetus.

More recently, clonazepam has also been recommended because of its particularly low teratogenic potential and longer half-life, compared to alprazolam (Cohen et al., 1989). Whenever possible, it is wise to urge the patient to utilize individual or group therapy to minimize the use of any medication. Until larger population-based studies disconfirm even the most minimal risk to the fetus, all medications must be prescribed with the greatest care. The human teratogenic potential of the nonbenzodiazepine anxiolytic buspirone is unknown; the benzodiazepines themselves have been reported to cause transient agitation, hypotonia, diminished respiration, low Apgar scores, difficulty with feeding and temperature regulation, and a neonatal abstinence syndrome (Cohen et al., 1989).

Finally, therapeutic abortions may lead to a host of psychiatric sequelae, including anxiety. The alert clinician should always have a high index of suspicion that the female patient of childbearing age who presents with a host of anxiety symptoms may be shrouding concerns about a recent or past elective abortion. Underlying shame, unresolved grief, or the toll taken by secret-keeping or deceptiveness (Lerner, 1993) may prove to be pivotal issues for the patient and therapist to wrestle with.

Clearly, sensitive case report series in the mode of Sichel, Cohen, Dimmock, and Rosenbaum (1993) will shed additional light on the role of anxiety in the reproductive cycle. In all likelihood, however, given the multifactorial nature of the etiology of anxiety disorders (Barsky, Barnett, & Cleary, 1994; Kendler, 1993; Liebowitz, 1993; Rosenbaum, Biederman, Pollack, & Hirshfeld, 1994; Shear, Cooper, Klerman, Busch, & Shapiro, 1993), care must be taken to describe the diverse populations who may be at risk, so that effective care can be provided and greater biopsychosocial understanding can be developed. Moreover, as mixed anxiety and depression syndromes are more thoroughly described (Frances, 1993; Liebowitz, 1993), we must also be alert to those who may have iatrogenically introduced depression, panic, and anxiety. Wagner and Berenson (1994), for example, described two women who developed major depression and panic disorder using the Norplant system for contraception.

There is also a high prevalence of anxiety symptoms among alcohol-dependent individuals (Schuckit & Hesselbrock, 1994), including women. Until more is known about the highly complex interactions between alcohol use and anxiety disorders, the practicing clinician is well advised to query patients with anxiety disorders about alcohol-dependent behavior and to counsel them adroitly with respect to childbearing practices, family history, and other comorbid psychiatric difficulties.

The role of trauma

In the past decade, the psychiatric literature has literally been flooded with reports of sexual and physical abuse in the case histories of women and of its concomitant effects on their psychological functioning (see Herman, 1992, and Waites, 1993, for thorough, systematic overviews). Not surprisingly, a host of reports are now emerging linking a variety of depressive and anxiety disorders with a history of posttraumatic stress disorder. These analyses work backward, retrospectively analyzing the prevalence of sexual and/or physical abuse in psychiatrically diagnosed patients. The findings are important not only for the challenging perspective they add to the etiology of anxiety and depression in women, but also for the revisionist picture they paint of contemporary neurobiological hypotheses related to anxiety.

Murrey et al. (1993) found that 43.7% of women with a depressive disorder and 48.5% of women with an anxiety disorder in their sample had a history of childhood sexual abuse. Murrey et al. were surprised to find such high rates of sexual abuse in female patients diagnosed with panic disorder, obsessive-compulsive disorder, major depression, and depressive disorder not otherwise specified. They argued that in view of the high prevalence of alleged abuse, clinicians must make routine sexual abuse screening a part of thorough history-taking and treatment planning. In another sample of 77 battered women, high rates of depression, anxiety, and overall distress were found (Kemp, Rawlings, & Green, 1991). A range of adverse experiences of inner-city life resulted in the increased incidence of anxiety in this high-risk population.

The effects of adult trauma, including a host of anxiety symptoms, were found in female Vietnam veterans (Furey, 1991) and in victims of political persecution (Fornazzari & Friere, 1990). In these groups of women who have been exposed to the stress of war and torture, respectively, numerous serious emotional, psychosocial, and other readjustment problems affecting their current functioning and quality of life persist for years after the etiological events. In addition to suggesting that mental health professionals must be aware of and understand the impact of all forms of trauma on women and the particular symptomatology from which they suffer, these studies show that those subjected to direct psychological and physical violence have a host of persistent symptoms, including pervasive anxiety and angst, that do not abate easily.

The life histories of these women, tragic and perplexing in their entirety, demonstrate how mental health professionals must take into account the role of trauma in the etiology of any serious emotional disturbance and must factor its role into a leavened approach to empathic understanding and therapeutic action. Thus both psychopharmacological and psychotherapeutic strategies must be tailored to fit the individual survivor of abuse, battering, torture, rape, or war, as new methods for intervention are rapidly but unpretentiously sought.

The roles of marriage and the family

A little more than a decade ago, a substantial number of reports in the family therapy literature emerged that linked agoraphobia in married women with specific conflicts and difficulties with their partners (Holm, 1982; Quadrio, 1984; Sable, 1991). This particular lens on the anxiety problem focused on marital issues that may inadvertently reinforce or support phobic conditions in women. Specifically, these findings suggest an environmental basis for some anxiety disorders, concluding that conflicts of separation/individuation or autonomy/dependency in each member of the dyad lead to agoraphobia.

For example, in some cases the husband may have a plethora of dependency anxieties himself. Via projective identification, he "deposits" his fears into his wife, who compliantly and submissively, but inadvertently and unconsciously, absorbs them. She becomes fearful of entering the outside world. The husband is thereby "protected" by the inability of the wife to effectively separate from him; a hostile dependency then develops where she becomes confined to her home, totally dependent and subjugated to him, but psychologically engaged in a marital dance where "husband and wife present a neat complementarity of needs—hers to bind herself in dependency, his to deny and project the same needs" (Quadrio, 1984, p. 170).

Interestingly, these case reports interdigitate with evolving genetic/twin studies as they also include glimpses into the lives of other family members. Indeed, the case histories are replete with depictions of other family members who suffer from agoraphobia or other anxiety disorders. Although the family dynamics suggest the need for ongoing exploration in a marital process or other form of individual treatment (e.g., insight-oriented dynamic psychotherapy), continuing systematic investigation will be needed to yield a greater sense of conviction about these convincing but idiosyncratic testimonials.

Likewise, research over the past 30 years has produced many reports linking child parental loss with adult depression and anxiety (Ainsworth, Blehar, Waters, & Wall, 1978; Bowlby, 1969, 1981). Theoretically, the actual physical presence of an attachment figure provides security; it enables children to explore and learn and provides them with a kind of psychological resilience against later psychiatric problems (Fonagy, Steele, Steele, Higgitt, & Target, 1994).

Defining the early risk factors for adult depressive and anxiety disorders is crucial to the mental health of both men and women. Emerging evidence now suggests that, in contrast to the widely held belief that death and loss figure prominently in later disorders, the quality of the relationship with the mother prior to later loss or separation (e.g., early attachment before age 6) contributes to later psychopathology (Bifulco, Harris, & Brown, 1992). Also crucial may be the endowed cognitive capacity of some children to deal with life stress. That is, some men and women may survive (and even thrive), despite extreme pathogenic life circumstances, because of an inherent capacity to self-reflect (Fonagy et al., 1994).

This ability permits the child to make use of those individuals available in the family or in other informal relationships. The capacity to reflect helps modify reactions to untoward, highly charged events. This hypothesis has far-reaching implications for psychotherapeutic practice and for psychiatric outcome studies of the anxiety disorders. Some individuals may have the notable capacity to make use of psychotherapeutic modalities to ameliorate their emotional distress. "Prescribing" certain psychotherapies (behavioral, cognitive, psychodynamic, group) may be predicated on the individual's capacity to use the particular form of treatment at a given point in life to "bring about a general facilitation of mental functioning" (Fonagy et al., 1994, p. 251).

In addition to bringing insight to bear on and serving as an emotional reservoir for noxious feeling states, the therapeutic encounter helps the individual deal with the trauma or life circumstances antecedent to the specific anxiety disorder. As the patient finds new anchors for life and new perspectives from which to view it, "thinking is facilitated and he or she can conceive of his or her world in new, more resilient and sometimes sadder and perhaps happier ways" (Fonagy et al., 1994, p. 251).

The survival advantage to anxiety and panic

Anxiety conveys an adaptive survival advantage to the individual. This almost universal state permits a man or woman to stay reasonably attuned to the environment and to potentially dangerous situations (Nesse, 1988; Zerbe, 1990). Moreover, individuals without a capacity to panic are at a survival disadvantage when confronted with situations of mortal danger (Nesse, 1988).

Anxiety disorders may be more common in women than in men because women are more closely attuned to the environment so that they can protect themselves and their children. The fear of unfamiliar situations regularly observed in patients with panic disorder may have its roots in incomplete resolution of conflicts related to dependence and independence (Shear et al., 1993); it may, however, also connote a survival advantage to women in an earlier time who, wandering from home, were at greater risk in both closed and open spaces. These are the same zones where animals are most vulnerable to entrapment and attack (Ballenger, 1989).

46

An integrated treatment model aimed at calming the individual who has hypersensitivity and an overdeveloped "alarm system" may thus be the treatment of choice for women whose anxiety thermostat is set too high for the modern environment. Although "evolutionary psychobiology cannot yet offer a confident explanation of panic" (Nesse, 1988, p. 482), it can provide a useful and supportive metaphor for patients who castigate themselves for their difficulties. Some clinicians use the psychotherapeutic technique of explaining the benefits conveyed by anxiety and panic and helping the patient avoid the most stressful life events and situations that make this paroxysmal disorder more likely. Manualized psychodynamically based treatment will help clinicians prove or refute these assertions and can be designed and conducted despite the inherent difficulties of complexity, compliance, and a belief that the best methods of treatment are already known. Clearly, a large subgroup of female patients is not being helped by current modalities: 40-55% of patients are treatment refractory after the withdrawal of psychotropic medications or other short-term, limited intervention strategies.

A final word on treatment

Despite the psychodynamic bias I have just alluded to, the real role of psychotropic medication in the anxiety disorders must also be highlighted. Although a thorough review goes well beyond the scope of this paper, it is important to acknowledge that women with anxiety have been treated with the usual range of benzodiazepines, non-benzodiazepine anxiolytics, tricyclic antidepressants, and selective serotonin reuptake inhibitor antidepressants (SSRIs).

Our knowledge of gender differences in pharmacokinetics and pharmacodynamics of these medications is as scant as the known gender differences in coronary vascular disease merely 5 years ago. Suffice it to say that women may be more likely to experience side effects when given medication because of altered plasma levels related to their larger proportion of body fat and the presence or absence of female gonadal hormones. Furthermore, medication may need adjustment during the premenstrual period, pregnancy, the postpartum period, and menopause.

Although the SSRIs and newer agents may hold great promise for women because these medications tend to have fewer side effects, women may also need to be monitored more closely with respect to dosage. Although most studies have yielded few gender differences with respect to higher plasma levels of the tricyclic antidepressants, some reports have substantiated that women occasionally have

47

higher plasma concentrations of these medications (Pajer, 1995; Preskorn & Mac, 1985). This rapidly evolving area of psychiatry requires that mental health professionals remain committed to continual immersion in the scientific literature. Only then can we provide our patients with the most sophisticated, up-to-date care and tailor their medicinal treatment to rapidly changing practice based on studies of gender-related dosage.

Finally, women's mental health treatment programs are assuming greater prominence in the health care system as they attempt to provide gender-sensitive care and evaluation. In general, women rate these programs highly (Lantican & Mayorga, 1993) because they emphasize a reduction in women's depressive and anxious symptomatologies by focusing on self-esteem, empowerment, tools to deal with and confront problematic life situations, and requests for an honest, straightforward appraisal of the program. Not surprisingly, the beneficial effects of individual psychotherapy are emphasized. The insights gained from describing one's life to an involved, empathic listener can never be underestimated (Herbst, 1992; Zerbe, 1993).

In addition to giving insight into the multifactorial nature of the illness, talking provides reassurance for the patient who feels ashamed and bewildered by her disorder. That reassurance may be the first psychological step in conquering anxiety. More important, it may serve as an affirming gesture to the woman who seeks to build a fuller sense of self in an "age of anxiety" that nevertheless holds the promise of unlimited possibility for both men and women.

References

Ainsworth, M.D.S., Blehar, M.C., Waters, E., & Wall, S. (1978). *Patterns of attachment: A psychological study of the strange situation.* Hillsdale, NJ: Erlbaum.

Applegarth, A. (1986). Women and work. In T. Bernay & D.W. Cantor (Eds.), *The psychology of today's woman: New psychoanalytic visions* (pp. 211-230). Hillsdale, NJ: Analytic Press.

Appignanesi, L., & Forrester, J. (1992). *Freud's women.* New York: BasicBooks.

Ballenger, J.C. (1989). Toward an integrated model of panic disorder. *American Journal of Orthopsychiatry, 59,* 284-293.

Barnett, R.C., & Baruch, G.K. (1978). Women in the middle years: A critique of research and theory. *Psychology of Women Quarterly, 3,* 187-197.

Barsky, A.J., Barnett, M.C., & Cleary, P.D. (1994). Hypochondriasis and panic disorder: Boundary and overlap. *Archives of General Psychiatry, 51,* 918-925.

Benedek, T. (1959). Parenthood as a developmental phase. *Journal of the American Psychoanalytic Association, 7,* 389-417.

Bifulco, A., Harris, T., & Brown, G.W. (1992). Mourning or early inadequate care? Reexamining the relationship of maternal loss in childhood with adult depression and anxiety. *Development and Psychopathology, 4,* 433-449.

Bowlby, J. (1969). *Attachment and loss: Vol. I. Attachment.* New York: Basic Books.

Bowlby, J. (1981). *Attachment and loss: Vol. III. Loss: Sadness and depression.* New York: Basic Books.

Brown, T.A., Barlow, D.H., & Liebowitz, M.R. (1994). The empirical basis of generalized anxiety disorder. *American Journal of Psychiatry, 151,* 1272-1280.

Brown, T.A., O'Leary, T.A., & Barlow, D.H. (1993). Generalized anxiety disorder. In D.H. Barlow (Ed.), *Clinical handbook of psychological disorders: A step-by-step treatment manual* (2nd ed., pp. 137-188). New York: Guilford.

Clark, N.M., Janz, N.K., Dodge, J., & Garrity, C. R. (1994). Managing heart disease: A study of experiences of older women. *Journal of the American Medical Women's Association, 49*(6), 202-206.

Cohen, L.S., Heller, V.L., & Rosenbaum, J.F. (1989). Treatment guidelines for psychotropic drug use in pregnancy. *Psychosomatics, 30,* 25-33.

Fonagy, P., Steele, M., Steele, H., Higgitt, A., & Target, M. (1994). The Emanuel Miller Memorial Lecture 1992: The theory and practice of resilience. *Journal of Child Psychology and Psychiatry and Allied Disciplines, 35,* 231-257.

Fornazzari, X., & Friere, M. (1990). Women as victims of torture. *Acta Psychiatrica Scandinavica, 82,* 257-260.

Frances, A.J. (1993). Introduction: Part I. Treatment strategies for complicated anxiety. *Journal of Clinical Psychiatry, 54*(5, Suppl), 3.

Fraser, A. (1984). *The weaker vessel.* New York: Knopf.

Furey, J.A. (1991). Women Vietnam veterans: A comparison of studies. *Journal of Psychosocial Nursing and Mental Health Services, 29*(3), 11-13.

Herbst, P.K.R. (1992). From helpless victim to empowered survivor: Oral history as a treatment for survivors of torture. *Women and Therapy, 13*(1-2), 141-154.

Herman, J.L. (1992). *Trauma and recovery.* New York: BasicBooks.

Holm, H.J. (1982). The agoraphobic married woman and her marriage pattern: A clinical study. In F.W. Kaslow (Ed.), *The international book of family therapy* (pp. 388-413). New York: Brunner/Mazel.

Horney, K. (1926). The flight from womanhood. *International Journal of Psycho-Analysis, 7,* 324-339.

Judd, L.L. (1994). Social phobia: A clinical overview. *Journal of Clinical Psychiatry, 55*(6, Suppl.), 5-9.

Judelson, D.R. (1994). Coronary heart disease in women: Risk factors and prevention. *Journal of the American Medical Women's Association, 49*(6), 186-191.

Kemp, A., Rawlings, E.I., & Green, B.L. (1991). Post-traumatic stress disorder (PTSD) in battered women: A shelter sample. *Journal of Traumatic Stress, 4,* 137-148.

Kendler, K.S. (1993). Twin studies of psychiatric illness: Current status and future directions. *Archives of General Psychiatry, 50,* 905-915.

Kendler, K.S., Neale, M.C., Kessler, R.C., Heath, A.C., & Eaves, L.J. (1992). Generalized anxiety disorder in women: A population-based twin study. *Archives of General Psychiatry, 49,* 267-272.

Kendler, K.S., Neale, M.C., Kessler, R.C., Heath, A.C., & Eaves, L.J. (1993). Panic disorder in women: A population-based twin study. *Psychological Medicine, 23,* 397-406.

Kestenberg, J.S. (1976). Regression and reintegration in pregnancy. *Journal of the American Psychoanalytic Association, 24*(Suppl.), 213-250.

Lantican, L.S., & Mayorga, J. (1993). Effectiveness of a women's mental health treatment program: A pilot study. *Mental Health Nursing, 14,* 31-49.

Lerner, H.G. (1993). *The dance of deception: Pretending and truth-telling in women's lives.* New York: HarperCollins.

Liebowitz, M.R. (1993). Mixed anxiety and depression: Should it be included in DSM-IV? *Journal of Clinical Psychiatry, 54*(5, Suppl.), 4-7.

Moulton, R. (1986). Professional success: A conflict for women. In J. Alpert (Ed.), *Psychoanalysis and women: Contemporary reappraisals* (pp. 161-182). Hillsdale, NJ: Analytic Press.

49

Murrey, G.J., Bolen, J., Miller, N., Sinensted, K., Robbins, M., & Truskowski, F. (1993). History of childhood sexual abuse in women with depressive and anxiety disorders: A comparison study. *Journal of Sex Education and Therapy, 19*(1), 13-19.

Nadelson, C.C. (1989). Issues in the analyses of single women in their thirties and forties. In J.M. Oldham & R.S. Liebert (Eds.), *The middle years: New psychoanalytic perspectives* (pp. 105-122). New Haven, CT: Yale University Press.

Nesse, R. M. (1988). Panic disorder: An evolutionary view. *Psychiatric Annals, 18,* 478-483.

Pajer, K. (1995). New strategies in the treatment of depression in women. *Journal of Clinical Psychiatry, 56*(Suppl. 2), 30-37.

Penn, L. (1986). The pregnant therapist: Transference and countertransference issues. In J. Alpert (Ed.), *Psychoanalysis and women: Contemporary reappraisals* (pp. 287-316). Hillsdale, NJ: Analytic Press.

Person, E.S. (1988). *Dreams of love and fateful encounters: The power of romantic passion.* New York: Norton.

Preskorn, S.H., & Mac, D.S. (1985). Plasma levels of amitriptyline: Effect of age and sex. *Journal of Clinical Psychiatry, 46,* 276-277.

Quadrio, C. (1984). Families of agoraphobic women. *Australian and New Zealand Journal of Psychiatry, 18,* 164-170.

Rosenbaum, J.F., Biederman, J., Pollock, R.A., & Hirshfeld, D.R. (1994). The etiology of social phobia. *Journal of Clinical Psychiatry, 55*(6, Suppl.), 10-16.

Roy-Byrne, P.P., & Cowley, D. S. (1988). Biological aspects [of panic disorders]. *Psychiatric Annals, 18,* 457-463.

Sable, P. (1991). Attachment, anxiety, and agoraphobia. *Women and Therapy, 11*(2), 55-69.

Schuckit, M.A., & Hesselbrock, V. (1994). Alcohol dependence and anxiety disorders: What is the relationship? *American Journal of Psychiatry, 151,* 1723-1734.

Shear, M.K., Cooper, A.M., Klerman, G.L., Busch, F.N., & Shapiro, T. (1993). A psychodynamic model of panic disorder. *American Journal of Psychiatry, 150,* 859-866.

Shorter, E. (1991). *From paralysis to fatigue: A history of psychosomatic illness in the modern era.* New York: Free Press.

Sichel, D.A., Cohen, L.S., Dimmock, J.A., & Rosenbaum, J.F. (1993). Postpartum obsessive compulsive disorder: A case series. *Journal of Clinical Psychiatry, 54,* 156-159.

Sichel, D.A., Cohen, L.S., Rosenbaum, J.F., & Driscoll, J. (1993). Postpartum onset of obsessive-compulsive disorder. *Psychosomatics, 34,* 277-279.

Wagner, K.D., & Berenson, A.B. (1994). Norplant-associated major depression and panic disorder. *Journal of Clinical Psychiatry, 55,* 478-480.

Waites, E.A. (1993). *Trauma and survival: Post-traumatic and dissociative disorders in women.* New York: Norton.

Wenger, N.K. (1994). Coronary heart disease in women: Gender differences in diagnostic evaluation. *Journal of the American Medical Women's Association, 49*(6), 181-185.

Wise, M.G., & Griffies, W.S. (1995). A combined treatment approach to anxiety in the medically ill. *Journal of Clinical Psychiatry, 56*(Suppl. 2), 14-19.

Zerbe, K.J. (1990). Through the storm: Psychoanalytic theory in the psychotherapy of the anxiety disorders. *Bulletin of the Menninger Clinic, 54,* 171-183.

Zerbe, K.J. (1993). *The body betrayed: Women, eating disorders, and treatment.* Washington, DC: American Psychiatric Press.

4. Anxiety and Addiction: A Clinical Perspective on Comorbidity

Robert L. DuPont, MD

Anxiety disorders and addictive disorders, the two most common mental disorders in the United States, come in a wide variety of clinical manifestations. They range in severity from relatively mild to incapacitating. Both are chronic disorders that typically wax and wane over patients' lifetimes.

Addiction and anxiety have been subject to increasing public and professional attention and have been topics of intense interest in biopsychiatry in recent years (Clark & Sayette, 1993; Kaplan, Sadock, & Grebb, 1994; Nunes, McGrath, & Quitkin, 1995; Ross, 1994). Both addiction and anxiety had previously been widely viewed as defects of character or as deficiencies of willpower, but they are now seen to have significant biological as well as psychosocial dimensions. They are different in that the role of medications is relatively minor in the treatment of addiction, while they play a major part in the treatment of anxiety disorders. Conversely, mutual-aid 12-step programs are central to addiction treatment but are seldom part of the treatment of anxiety.

Comorbidity

A growing body of evidence, based on the landmark Epidemiologic Catchment Area (ECA) study begun in 1984, has demonstrated not only that addiction and anxiety are prevalent and often comorbid, but also that the overlap is greater than would be expected if their relationship were purely random (Weissman, 1988). The anxiety disorders have a lifetime prevalence in the ECA data of 14.7%, compared to a lifetime prevalence of 16.7% for any substance use disorder. Of those with anxiety disorders, 23.7% also meet diagnostic criteria for substance use disorders at some time in their lifetime.

During their lifetimes, people with anxiety disorders are 1.7 times more likely than those without anxiety disorders to suffer from a substance use disorder (Regier et al., 1990). The odds ratios for anxiety disorders range from 1.6 for phobias and 2.5 for obsessive-compulsive disorder to 2.9 for panic disorder. For perspective on this connection, the odds ratio for any affective disorder is 2.6 and for bipolar

Dr. DuPont is the president of the Institute for Behavior and Health, Inc., Rockville, Maryland.

disorder is 6.6, which shows that the affective disorders are somewhat more closely linked to substance use disorders than are the anxiety disorders (Brown et al., 1995).

With respect to which is more prevalent, anxiety or addiction, the lifetime rates are highest for addiction, but the 6-month prevalence is 8.9% for anxiety disorders and 6.1% for any substance use disorder. Thus addiction has a higher lifetime prevalence but a lower 6-month prevalence than the anxiety disorders. Alcohol problems are about twice as prevalent in all time periods as are all other drug-use problems combined (Regier et al., 1990).

Although the ECA data show a substantial level of comorbidity between the anxiety and the substance use disorders, it is equally important to note that nearly three fourths of people with an anxiety disorder never suffer from a substance use disorder. Conversely, 80.3% of people with a diagnosis of alcohol abuse or dependence never meet criteria for an anxiety disorder. Among people with a diagnosis of other drug abuse or dependence, 71.7% never meet diagnostic criteria for an anxiety disorder (Regier et al., 1990).

When it comes to comorbidity with substance use disorders, the most tightly linked diagnosis studied in the ECA sample was antisocial personality disorder, which had an odds ratio of 29.6, with about 84% of people with that diagnosis meeting diagnostic criteria for a substance use disorder during their lifetime. Only about 14% of people with a substance use disorder suffered from antisocial personality disorder. Overall, the ECA study found that approximately 60% of people with a mental disorder experienced two or more diagnosable disorders in their lifetime. Because the ECA data come from studies in five communities rather than from a national sample, and because the data are now more than a decade old, the ECA study's findings have been questioned (Robins & Regier, 1991).

More recently, the National Comorbidity Survey (NCS) from the University of Michigan has explored the high rate of comorbidity found in the ECA data, providing valuable new information on the linkages of various diagnoses. In this national sample of noninstitutionalized Americans ages 15-54 who responded to a structured diagnostic interview, 24.9% meet diagnostic criteria for an anxiety disorder during their lifetime and 26.6% meet diagnostic criteria for a substance use disorder (Kessler et al., 1994).

The NCS study found that about 40% of subjects with a 12-month substance use disorder also experience a mental disorder during that period, and that 14.7% of subjects with a mental disorder also meet criteria for a recent substance use disorder. Surprisingly, 79.3% of those with lifetime comorbidity for substance use and any anxiety disorder reported that the mental disorder occurred first. The median age of onset of mental disorders was 12 years. The onset of the substance use disorders typically occurs in middle or late adolescence (average age 21 years) (Kessler et al., in press). The NCS study did not capture data on the occurrence of obsessive-compulsive disorder. Regarding 12-month comorbidity rates for any substance use disorder with the affective and anxiety disorders, the NCS findings indicated that 35.6% of subjects with any substance use disorder have an anxiety disorder; of those with any anxiety disorder, 15.2% also experience a substance use disorder during the prior 12 months (see Table 1).

Looked at more generally, the NCS data give a picture of the overlap of broad diagnostic groups showing that 37.8% of people with a nonsubstance use mental disorder are comorbid for a substance use disorder. Conversely, 64.7% of people with an alcohol use disorder are comorbid for either a drug or a nonsubstance use mental disorder, and 88.3% of those with another drug use disorder are comorbid for either mental or alcohol use disorders (see Figure 1).

Characterizing the connections

Anxiety and addiction have many overlaps (Brady & Lydiard, 1993; Kushner, Sher, & Beitman, 1990; Linnoila, 1989; Schuckit & Hesselbrock, 1994). The first connection is that both are highly prevalent, so that there is a substantial random comorbidity. Second, alcohol and other drug use can cause anxiety through a variety of mechanisms broadly defined as resulting from intoxication and withdrawal. Examples include panic disorder triggered by drug use, such as marijuana- or LSD-induced panic attacks. Alcohol and other drug withdrawal is a common cause of acute anxiety, including panic attacks.

Third, anxiety can cause addiction through several mechanisms, including using alcohol and other drugs nonmedically to reduce anxiety-caused distress, as well as effects on the lifestyle of affected people. A person with a social phobia may be more likely to drink to overcome social anxiety, or a drug addict may be more socially isolated and thus more prone to experience agoraphobic symptoms. Fourth, the connection between addiction and anxiety may extend to the children of people suffering from addiction and anxiety, because both have a genetic component. For example, children of addicted people may be more likely to have anxiety problems than children of nonaddicted people (Cloninger, 1987; Schuckit, 1994). Fifth, the connection between addiction and anxiety may occur through the medications or other treatments used to manage one or the other of these

Table 1. *Conditional probabilities of 12-month comorbidities between NCS/DSM-III-R mental disorders and substance abuse*

	ANY SUB	
	S	M
Affective		
Major depressive episode	22.9	18.4
Dysthymia	2.4	18.8
Mania	1.7	37.1
Any	24.5	18.3
Anxiety		
Generalized anxiety disorder	8.1	21.0
Panic disorder (with/without agoraphobia)	4.5	16.0
Posttraumatic stress disorder	8.3	17.7
Social phobia	16.6	17.4
Simple phobia	14.5	13.5
Agoraphobia	8.4	17.7
Any	35.6	15.2
Any mental disorder		
One+	42.7	14.7
Three+	12.8	23.6

Note: ANY SUB = abuse and/or dependence on alcohol and/or drugs. One+ = one or more mental disorders. Three+ = three or more comorbid mental disorders. Coefficients in the columns labeled S are proportions of respondents with the substance use disorder in the column who also had the 12-month mental disorder in the corresponding row. For example, 22.9% of NCS respondents with 12-month ANY SUB also had at least one major depressive episode in the same 12-month period. Coefficients in the columns labeled M are proportions of respondents with the mental disorder in the corresponding row who also had the substance use disorder in the corresponding column. For example, 18.4 % of NCS respondents with a 12-month major depressive episode also met criteria for 12-month ANY SUB.

(Adapted from: Kessler, R.C., Nelson, C.B., McGonagle, K.A., Edlund, M.J., Frank, R.G., & Leaf, P.J. [in press]. The epidemiology of co-occurring mental disorders and substance use disorders in the National Comorbidity Survey: Implications for prevention and service utilization. Reprinted, with permission, from the *American Journal of Orthopsychiatry.* Copyright © by the American Orthopsychiatric Association, Inc.)

groups of disorders. In particular, the use of controlled substances to treat anxiety in addicted people may cause or contribute to addictive disease. When it comes to the treatment of anxiety disorders, the greatest concern centers on the use of benzodiazepines in the treatment of panic and other anxiety symptoms (DuPont & Saylor, 1991). Most clinicians have seen examples of all five of these connections between addiction and anxiety disorders (see Table 2).

With respect to the treatment of patients with comorbid addiction

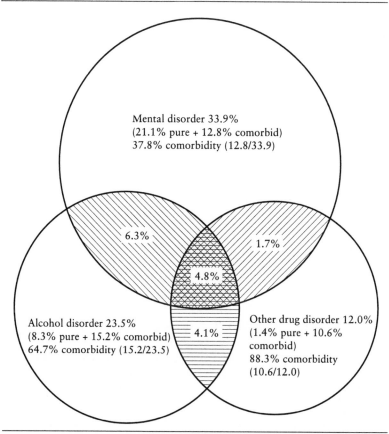

Figure 1. *Lifetime prevalence of comorbid mental and addictive disorders in the United States, noninstitutionalized household population ages 15-54, 1990.* (From: Kessler, R.C., Edlund, M.J., Frank, R.G., Kendler, K.S., Leaf, P.J., Nelson, C.B., & Wittchen, H.-U. [1995]. *Comorbidity of DSM-III-R mental disorders and substance disorders in the National Comorbidity Survey.* Manuscript submitted for publication. Reprinted with permission of the authors.)

Table 2. *Connections between addiction and anxiety*

1. Random association of common disorders.
2. Anxiety caused by alcohol and other drug use.
3. Anxiety-caused addiction.
4. Children of parents with one class of disorder may be more likely to experience the other disorder.
5. Medicines used to treat addiction may cause or exacerbate addiction.

and anxiety, the 12-step programs often play a vital role (DuPont, 1994). Patients with comorbid conditions present a greater therapeutic challenge and often have a poorer prognosis than patients with a single diagnosis (Kessler et al., 1994).

Self-medication and physical dependence

To manage addicted and anxious patients, clinicians must learn to distinguish between medical and nonmedical use of potentially abused substances. Although alcohol no longer has any medical uses, many potentially abused drugs do have widespread medical uses, including the opioid analgesics, stimulants, and the benzodiazepines. Addicted patients sometimes use controlled substances prescribed by physicians as part of their addictive substance use.

Compounding the confusion when comorbidity exists over which is the primary disorder (addiction or anxiety), physicians sometimes explain their patients' use of alcohol and other drugs as "self-medication" (Kushner et al., 1990). Tobacco use by the mentally ill has been defined as self-medication to oppose the imposition of smoke-free rules in hospitals (Foderaro, 1995). The concept of self-medication blurs the distinction between medical and nonmedical substance use. To make sound clinical and policy decisions, clinicians must keep these distinctions clear. Medical and nonmedical substance use can be distinguished on five variables (see Table 3). Self-medication with alcohol and other drugs nonmedically does not fit these five criteria for medical use. Self-medication does fit the criteria for nonmedical use.

Table 3. *Separating medical from nonmedical use*

	Medical use	Nonmedical use
Intent	To treat diagnosed illness	To party or to "treat" distressing effects of alcohol or other drug abuse
Effect	Makes life of user better	Makes life of user worse
Pattern	Stable, medically sensible	Unstable, usually high dose
Control	Shared honestly with physician	Self-controlled
Legality	Legal	Illegal (except alcohol use by adults)

The concept of self-medication ensnares the clinician and the patient in a potentially unhealthy justification of addiction. What is called self-medication is usually addictive behavior dressed up in a medical disguise. Addicted people use their addictive substances not only to get high but also to ease discomfort from many sources, including illnesses (such as anxiety disorders), and from withdrawal states and other adverse effects that are a result of their addictive substance use. Patients who are addicted to nicotine, alcohol, and other drugs need help to completely stop their use of these substances. They do not benefit from medical justifications for their addictive substance use, even though stopping such use often is temporarily uncomfortable.

A second distinction needs to be made in sorting out the confusion in the treatment of people who are comorbid for addiction and anxiety disorders. Addiction must be distinguished from physical dependence. It is common for nonaddicted clinically anxious patients to be physically dependent on medications, including benzodiazepines, without showing any manifestations of addiction (Sellers et al., 1993) (see Table 4).

Anxious patients taking therapeutic, or even very low, doses of benzodiazepines regularly self-report that they are "addicted" to their medications because they feel more anxious when they stop using them. Such admissions reflect the common misunderstanding of the nature of addiction and, when accepted at face value, complicate

Table 4. *Separating addiction from physical dependence*

Addiction
> Loss of control, continued use despite problems caused by use
> Denial, dishonesty
> Relapse is common
> A complex, progressive, malignant, biopsychosocial, lifelong, potentially fatal disease
> Not a complication of medical treatment unless there is a prior history of addiction to alcohol and other drugs
> Best treated by specific addiction treatment and 12-step fellowships

Physical dependence
> A cellular adaptation of the continuous presence of a biologically active substance
> Withdrawal symptoms on abrupt discontinuation
> Not associated with relapse
> A benign, temporary problem
> Common to many substances used in medicine, including steroids, antidepressants, antiepilepsy, and antihypertensive medicines
> Best treated by gradual dose reduction

the patient's treatment and even cause inappropriate admission to an addiction treatment program. Patients who experience withdrawal symptoms (heightened anxiety and insomnia) when they sharply reduce their doses or stop their use of benzodiazepines need to be educated that this is a normal and temporary problem unrelated to addiction, and that it can be managed medically by a gradual dose reduction so that the brain can get used to functioning without the benzodiazepines. If patients are not educated and supported in their efforts to discontinue benzodiazepine use, they can feel confused, guilty, angry, and frightened as they begin to think of themselves as "addicted" or "hooked" on their medication (Lader, 1990).

The cognitive approach to withdrawal symptoms is helpful to anxious patients because it removes the frightening meaning of the upsurge of symptoms through education and active support from their physicians (DuPont, 1990b). The return of anxiety after the discontinuation of a benzodiazepine is not a sign of dependence on the benzodiazepine. It is a manifestation of the enduring, underlying anxiety disorder. I find it helpful to compare my use of glasses for myopia to appropriate medical use of benzodiazepines to treat anxiety disorders: Take away my glasses and I experience distress, including anxiety and "glasses-seeking behavior." This intense discomfort does not mean that I am "addicted" to my glasses.

Some patients who are addicted to alcohol and other drugs do become addicted to benzodiazepines given for the treatment of anxiety disorders. They use the benzodiazepines *along with* alcohol and other drugs taken nonmedically, often in unstable and high doses. Such addicted patients, whose use of benzodiazepines is clearly nonmedical, need addiction treatment, not reassurance about the benign nature of physical dependence (DuPont, 1990d, 1990e).

Unless these distinctions between medical and nonmedical use and between addiction and physical dependence are made, two potentially serious errors occur in the treatment of addicted and anxious patients (DuPont & DuPont, 1994). The first error, which is common, is to prescribe controlled substances to actively addicted patients, often worsening their addiction. The second error, which is even more common, is to withhold safe and effective treatment with controlled substances from nonaddicted anxious patients out of misplaced fear of addiction (Wilford, 1990).

Managing comorbidity

Although the use of narcotic analgesics and stimulants in outpatient settings by people who are addicted to alcohol and other drugs can be a serious problem, it is relatively uncommon (Hill, 1990). Far more common is the use of benzodiazepines on an outpatient basis for people who are relatively stable but who continue to drink alcohol and/or use drugs nonmedically in ways that may create problems in their lives (DuPont, 1990c). Physicians who prescribe benzodiazepines may not take a history of addiction, so they never find out about the comorbidity of addiction and anxiety problems. At other times, patients distort the facts or lie outright to their physicians to hide their addictive use of alcohol and/or other drugs (DuPont & Saylor, 1991).

Because addicted people typically use benzodiazepines in ways that are different from how nonaddicted patients use medications, if a patient has been using a benzodiazepine, that patient's own experience with the medication is a good measure of addiction. Addictive use of benzodiazepines commonly involves the goal of getting high. Because tolerance to both the sedative and euphoric effects develops rapidly after a few doses, patients who seek these effects must use the benzodiazepines at high and unstable doses and/or add other substances (most often alcohol, marijuana, or cocaine) to get the desired euphoric effect.

When a patient takes a relatively low and stable dose of the benzodiazepine over a prolonged period and does not add other potentially abusable substances, the behavior reliably signals nonaddictive, or medical, benzodiazepine use. Nonaddicted patients taking a benzodiazepine medically seek its antipanic and antianxiety effects, not its euphoric effects. Because tolerance does not develop to these medical effects, even with benzodiazepine use over many years, these patients do not escalate their intake. Most anxious patients using benzodiazepines do not use alcohol at all. Clinically anxious patients without a prior history of addiction who do use alcohol typically do not have an alcohol-related problem, and they drink alcohol sparingly.

Patients addicted to alcohol and other drugs may use benzodiazepines to mitigate the adverse effects of their nonmedical use of alcohol or other drugs. In these cases, the benzodiazepine use is not always at a high dose, but it takes place in the context of the addictive use of alcohol and/or other drugs. Typical examples of this pattern are the use of benzodiazepines to treat insomnia and morning hangovers associated with alcohol and cocaine use or the withdrawal symptoms experienced by heroin users. Such benzodiazepine use, sometimes mislabeled "self-medication," is nonmedical because it is linked directly to the abuse of alcohol or other drugs taken nonmedically. For patients who have been using a benzodiazepine for some time, I use a simple four-part checklist to identify addiction or other problems (see Table 5).

When treating a patient for addiction, clinicians should consider the possibility of an anxiety disorder only after the patient is clean and sober for several months or longer. Treaters should also consider the effects of nicotine and caffeine, because many addicted patients are heavy users of these anxiety-producing substances. Patients who are comorbid for addiction and anxiety should be treated like any other person with an anxiety disorder, except for the use of benzodiazepines and for insistence on achieving abstinence from alcohol and other nonmedical drugs. If the clinician and the comorbid patient choose to use a benzodiazepine to treat the anxiety disorder, it should be done after careful consideration of the risks associated with that use and only after discussing the treatment with the patient's spouse or another family member, and with the sponsor if the patient is participating in Alcoholics Anonymous (AA) or Narcotics Anonymous (NA). If a benzodiazepine is prescribed for a recovering alcoholic or drug addict, one with a relatively low abuse potential should be considered, such as oxazepam or clonazepam, rather than one with a higher abuse potential, such as alprazolam, lorazepam, and diazepam (Baron, Sands, Ciraulo, & Shader, 1990; DuPont, 1988).

When treating for anxiety, clinicians should consider the potential for comorbid addiction to alcohol and other drugs. Given that about one fourth of people with anxiety disorders have a diagnosable substance use disorder at some time in their lives, it is helpful to take an addiction history from all anxiety disorder patients. The first requirement in an evaluation is to ask patients about their use of alcohol and other drugs. Taking more than three or four drinks of alcohol a week and using any illegal drug in the prior year should raise concern about the possibility of active addiction. An interview with a family member often helps to establish the diagnosis of addiction or to rule it out. To identify a patient's current illicit drug use, clinicians may find it useful to administer a urine or a hair test (DuPont & Baumgartner, 1995).

A simple technique to identify alcohol abuse in routine clinical practice is to use the CAGE test. Patients can be asked whether they have ever tried to *Cut* down their alcohol or other drug use, whether they have ever gotten *Angry* with anyone who suggested they stop using alcohol or other drugs (especially their spouse or physician), whether they have ever felt *Guilty* about use of either alcohol or other drugs, and whether they have ever drunk alcohol or used drugs as an *Eye-opener* early in the day. Even one positive response is a strong indicator of a problem, while three or four positive responses are diagnostic of addictive disease (Ewing, 1984).

Table 5. *Benzodiazepine checklist to assess reasonableness of continued treatment*

1. *Problem being treated*
Does the patient's diagnosis justify continued treatment with a benzodiazepine? Has the patient significantly benefited from this treatment?
2. *Benzodiazepine use*
Does the patient's use of the benzodiazepine remain within the prescribed limits and duration of treatment? Has the patient avoided the nonmedical use of other prescribed or nonprescribed potentially addictive substances, including alcohol used to excess?
3. *Toxic behavior*
Has the patient been free of any signs of intoxication or impairment from the use of the benzodiazepine medication, either alone or in combination with alcohol or other drugs?
4. *Family monitor*
Does the patient's family monitor confirm that there have been no problems with the benzodiazepine use and that the patient has benefited from the use of the medication?

A "no" on any of these questions indicates a potentially serious problem and may justify cessation of benzodiazepine use.

A "yes" on all four questions is common for nonaddicted anxious patients receiving a benzodiazepine and generally justifies continued use of the medicine if both patient and physician consider this a wise course of action.

In difficult cases, or when there are doubts about the existence of a comorbid condition with which the clinician is not familiar, the treater should not hesitate to consult a colleague for an evaluation (Barnes, Aronson, & Delbanco, 1987). Many physicians who are expert at addiction medication are not familiar with the treatment of anxiety disorders, and many physicians who are expert with anxiety disorders are not comfortable with addicted patients.

The most alarming case of comorbidity of addiction and anxiety is a patient being treated for anxiety with a benzodiazepine who escalates the dose of the benzodiazepine while also using alcohol and/or other controlled substances (most often stimulants and narcotic analgesics) on an outpatient basis in a pattern that undermines the patient's functional abilities in major life areas, including family and work (Miller, 1994). Prescribing physicians who use controlled substances for outpatients should have a high index of suspicion for addiction and a well-thought-out plan for intervention when it occurs, because this problem occurs sometime in virtually every physician's practice. Having an open line of communication with the patient and the patient's family permits the relatively early recognition of these problems and facilitates interventions.

Benzodiazepines in the treatment of anxiety disorders

Many physicians do not prescribe benzodiazepines for anxiety because (as with prescribing narcotic analgesics and stimulants) they are concerned that their patients may become addicted to prescribed controlled substances. Physicians may also be uncertain about their own ability to identify addiction when it develops. Patients who are suffering from an anxiety disorder need education about the nature of their disorder and their treatment options, including the use of cognitive-behavioral treatment, supportive psychotherapy, and medications (especially the antidepressants and the benzodiazepines) (Barlow, 1988; DuPont 1986, 1992a, 1992b; DuPont & Saylor, 1992). Self-help options should be considered (Saylor, DuPont, & Brouillard, 1990). Because both addiction and anxiety disorders are family diseases, many patients have family experiences, as well as personal experiences, with several treatment alternatives. With this background, patients often have a good idea of what works and what does not work for them (DuPont, 1992c).

In going through the treatment options, I contrast the benzodiazepines with the antidepressants used to treat anxiety disorders, noting that the benzodiazepines have some advantages and some disadvantages. The major advantages are that they produce fewer side effects than the antidepressants, and that they offer the option of either everyday use or as-needed use. Because the anxiety disorders tend to wax and wane over time, it is often attractive to patients to have a medication that they can take only when they need it. Many patients find it helpful to be able to adjust their dose up or down depending on their needs, which can be done with the benzodiazepines because of the short latency between taking the dose and experiencing the therapeutic benefit. In contrast, the antidepressants, when used to treat anxiety disorders, have a long latency between changes in dose and therapeutic effects, making dose adjustments over short periods of time not helpful in dealing with short-term shifts in the level of anxiety.

The benzodiazepines have the disadvantage of needing to be taken 2-4 times a day when taken on an everyday basis, rather than once a day as most antidepressants are. In addition, the benzodiazepines may produce withdrawal symptoms on discontinuation (DuPont et al., 1992). Abrupt discontinuation from fairly high doses can even lead to epileptic seizures. The benzodiazepines can also be abused by people with active addiction, and in some cases they cause problems for patients recovering from addiction to alcohol and other drugs.

Because anxiety disorders are usually lifelong, and because no treatment is likely to end anxiety problems permanently, the choice of treatment, including the choice of a particular medication, is not a high-stakes, high-pressure decision. It is a decision that the patient and the physician can make over time, trying first one approach and then another in seeking the best fit for each patient's needs at particular times. The treatment of anxiety disorders is not like surgery, where it is hard to reverse the decision once an incision has been made. If problems develop—and they may—in taking medications for anxiety disorders, it is relatively easy to make adjustments and to try another course of action.

Any side effects that may develop with any medication for anxiety, including a benzodiazepine, are eliminated when the medication is stopped. This perspective is often helpful for anxious patients because it makes the choice of treatment less frightening and sets up long-term collaboration involving active roles for both patients and physicians. When this picture is sketched out, many clinically anxious patients choose to use one of the benzodiazepines, often finding great help from these generally safe and well-understood medications (DuPont, 1988).

Treating addicted patients who also suffer from an anxiety disorder requires a different approach when it comes to using a benzodiazepine (Frances & Borg, 1993; Roth, 1989). Many of these patients are reluctant to use any brain-affecting medications. They see all psychoactive medications, including the benzodiazepines and the antidepressants, as "mood altering" and therefore as off-limits to them in their recovery. I explain that this approach is fine, because it is not mandatory for them to use medications in the treatment of their anxiety disorders. In this regard, the treatment of anxiety disorders is not like that of some other illnesses (e.g., severe diabetes requires insulin).

The standard question I ask recovering patients who have anxiety disorders to consider is their own long-term self-interest. What treatments produce the best quality of life for them? If they are able to use nonpharmacological treatments and to live full, normal lives without undue suffering and without limitations as a result of their anxiety disorder, then they surely do not need medication. On the other hand, if they continue to suffer and if they have limitations in their lives as a result of their anxiety disorder, then medication may be appropriate, at least on a trial basis. With addicted patients, I distinguish between controlled substances and noncontrolled substances, and I define the syndrome of addiction as separate from physical dependence.

A similar discussion can be useful for patients who have no history of addiction but who share the aversion to the use of medication, usually because they believe that they should be able to overcome their anxiety disorders with willpower or psychotherapy. Using medication makes them feel like a failure. For these patients, as for many recovering addicts, the resistance to all medication is typically based on fear, often fear of addiction. It is useful to provide realistic education to fearful patients without either minimizing the risks or exaggerating the benefits that may result from the use of medication to treat anxiety disorders.

It is seldom necessary to use a benzodiazepine in the treatment of recovering patients who also have an anxiety disorder, because other medications that have no abuse potential are effective (DuPont, 1992c), but there are times when anxiety disorder patients in stable recovery do benefit from the use of a benzodiazepine. In these cases, I involve patients' families and their sponsors in AA or NA in the decision to use benzodiazepines and in monitoring this use. When using an antidepressant for anxiety in patients who are comorbid for addiction and anxiety, it is sometimes useful to choose one of the more sedating antidepressants to reduce insomnia and daytime anxiety. The only antidepressant that has been reported to be abused by addicted patients is amitriptyline, so this medication should usually be avoided with comorbid patients (Cantor, 1979; Cohen, Hanbury, & Stimmel, 1978).

Because addicted patients in recovery are likely to encounter negative reactions to their use of benzodiazepines in their AA or NA meetings, I suggest that they not mention their use of these medications in such meetings. I remind them that it is essential that they be fully honest with their physicians, families, and sponsors, including telling all the facts about their benzodiazepine use. I have seldom seen a problem when these guidelines are followed, although on several occasions clinically anxious patients whom I considered to be using their benzodiazepines responsibly later defined their benzodiazepine use as problematic for their sobriety and took a dim view of my approach.

Workplace drug tests

Drug testing has become common in the American workplace, with 87% of large companies reporting some drug testing (American Management Association, 1994). Although federally mandated testing identifies only five drug classes (opiates, cocaine, marijuana, amphetamine/methamphetamine, and PCP), some employers also test for barbiturates and benzodiazepines (U.S. Department of Health and Human Services, 1988a). Current medical review officer (MRO) guidelines mandate that patients receiving medications under valid prescriptions be reported to their employers as "negative." Some employers doing nonregulated workplace drug testing do not use an MRO (U.S. Department of Health and Human Services, 1988b).

It is possible but rare for patients taking a benzodiazepine legitimately to be falsely accused of being a drug abuser under these circumstances. Antidepressants and other noncontrolled substances used to treat anxious patients are not identified on workplace drug tests. Patients who are subject to workplace drug testing, whether using controlled substances or not, are often worried that drug tests will reveal their medical treatment to their employer. They benefit from a clear and practical explanation of these processes and from the willingness of their physicians to help them with their employer if any problems emerge as a result of a poor employer program (DuPont, 1990a). Any physician concerned about a patient's treatment by an employer should contact a certified medical review officer for assistance.*

Guidelines for clinicians

Here are four practical guidelines for managing addicted and clinically anxious patients:

1. *Individualize the treatment plan.* Patients in the real world are complex and varied. When it comes to the treatment of both addictions and anxiety disorders, one approach does not fit all patients. This means that taking a careful history with consideration for comorbidity is essential for the treatment of all patients with either addictions or anxiety disorders. Development of a personalized treatment plan should take into consideration all the illnesses suffered by the patient, including addiction, anxiety, and other psychiatric as well as nonpsychiatric disorders.

2. *First things first: Stop nonmedical drug use.* When patients are addictively using alcohol or other drugs, whether or not they suffer from an anxiety disorder, the first priority is to achieve an alcohol- and drug-free state. A meaningful diagnosis of an anxiety disorder can be made only when a patient is free of the intoxicating effects of addicting substances and free of the symptoms of acute and protracted abstinence (Brown, Irwin, & Schuckit, 1991). Psychiatric

---

*Lists of certified medical review officers can be obtained from the Medical Review Certification Council (MRCC), 55 West Seegers Road, Arlington Heights, IL 60005, telephone (708) 228-7476; and the American Association of Medical Review Officers (AAMRO), PO Box 12873, Research Triangle Park, NC 27709, telephone (800) 489-1839.

pathology will frequently diminish in severity or even vanish when sobriety is achieved for more than a few months (De Soto, O'Donnell, & De Soto, 1989). Patients who are examined by their physicians while they are using alcohol and other drugs nonmedically or in the immediate postuse period, and who report that they have a prior history of anxiety and other mental disorders, must be treated cautiously because the past often looks quite different to addicted people once they are in stable recovery (Atkinson, Slater, Patterson, Grant, & Garfin, 1991; Morrissey & Schuckit, 1978).

3. *Do not use controlled substances for actively addicted outpatients.* Do not treat addicts who are actively using alcohol and other drugs with controlled substances on an outpatient basis because there is a risk that the controlled substances will be swept up into the addictive disease. However, there are some exceptions to this general rule.

Use of a benzodiazepine or another controlled substance must be monitored for all patients to ensure that dose levels remain within the usual therapeutic range and that no negative effects are seen in a patient's behavior. Working with family members is often helpful in monitoring such use. A common clinical dilemma is a clinically anxious patient who drinks alcohol in a stable maintenance drinking pattern, and who does not have negative physical or behavioral consequences of the drinking, but who refuses to enter addiction treatment. Under such circumstances, patients may receive benefit from modest doses of a benzodiazepine, but the risks are high and the benefits are usually low. Such an approach is therefore not only hazardous, but also usually unwise (as well as unnecessary).

4. *Avoid the "self-medication" trap.* Do not get caught in the rationalization that either the patient's nonmedical use of prescribed medications or the use of alcohol or other drugs is self-medication for anxiety or another disorder. Medical treatment must be honest and open, with the physician fully informed about the treatment and all of the patient's use of alcohol and other drugs. The medication must make the patient's life better. Self-medication fails on both counts: It is neither honest nor does it improve the patient's life. Patients do not self-medicate with antianxiety medications that do not produce a "high" or a reward. They only self-medicate with abusable and therefore controlled substances. This simple fact exposes the fallacy of the self-medication hypothesis.

Summary

Although addiction and anxiety are sometimes comorbid, approximately three fourths of patients with either diagnosis never experience the other. Confusion about addiction and anxiety can complicate the treatment of both conditions. An open, honest approach to these disorders will usually prevent or solve problems. Although the benzodiazepines are a particularly challenging aspect of the interaction of addiction and anxiety, it is important for the welfare of patients that these useful medications not be taken out of the therapeutic armamentarium because of misunderstanding about their roles in addiction and anxiety.

References

American Management Association. (1994). *1994 AMA survey on workplace drug testing and drug abuse policies*. New York: American Management Association.

Atkinson, J.H., Slater, M.A., Patterson, T.L., Grant, I., & Garfin, S.R. (1991). Prevalence, onset, and risk of psychiatric disorders in men with chronic low back pain: A controlled study. *Pain, 45,* 111-121.

Barlow, D.H. (1988). *Anxiety and its disorders: The nature and treatment of anxiety and panic.* New York: Guilford.

Barnes, H.N., Aronson, M.D., & Delbanco, T.L. (Eds.). (1987). *Alcoholism: A guide for the primary care physician.* New York: Springer-Verlag.

Baron, D.H., Sands, B.F., Ciraulo, D.A., & Shader, R.I. (1990). The diagnosis and treatment of panic disorder in alcoholics: Three cases. *American Journal of Drug and Alcohol Abuse, 16,* 287-295.

Brady, K.T., & Lydiard, R.B. (1993). The association of alcoholism and anxiety. *Psychiatric Quarterly, 64,* 135-149.

Brown, S.A., Inaba, R.K., Gillin, J.C., Schuckit, M.A., Stewart, M.A., & Irwin, M.R. (1995). Alcoholism and affective disorder: Clinical course of depressive symptoms. *American Journal of Psychiatry, 152,* 45-52.

Brown, S.A., Irwin, M., & Schuckit, M.A. (1991). Changes in anxiety among abstinent male alcoholics. *Journal of Studies on Alcohol, 52,* 55-61.

Cantor, R. (1979). Methadone maintenance and amitriptyline [Letter to the editor]. *Journal of the American Medical Association, 241,* 2378.

Clark, D.B., & Sayette, M.A. (1993). Anxiety and the development of alcoholism: Clinical and scientific issues. *American Journal on Addictions, 2,* 59-76.

Cloninger, C.R. (1987, April 24). Neurogenetic adaptive mechanisms in alcoholism. *Science, 236,* 410-416.

Cohen, M.J., Hanbury, R., & Stimmel, B. (1978). Abuse of amitriptyline. *Journal of the American Medical Association, 240,* 1372-1373.

De Soto, C.B., O'Donnell, W.E., & De Soto, J.L. (1989). Long-term recovery in alcoholics. *Alcoholism: Clinical and Experimental Research, 13,* 693-697.

DuPont, R.L. (1986). *Phobias and panic: A physician's guide to modern treatments.* Rockville, MD: The Phobia Society of America.

DuPont, R.L. (Ed.). (1988). Abuse of benzodiazepines: The problems & the solutions. *American Journal of Drug and Alcohol Abuse, 14*(Suppl 1).

DuPont, R.L. (1990a). Medicines and drug testing in the workplace: Therapeutic drugs and drugs of abuse in the era of the drug-free workplace. *Journal of Psychoactive Drugs, 22,* 451-459.

DuPont, R.L. (1990b). *A patient's guide to getting off a benzodiazepine.* Rockville, MD: DuPont Associates, P.A.

DuPont, R.L. (1990c). Policy concerns: Addiction, anxiety and benzodiazepines: A public policy perspective. In B.B. Wilford (Ed.), *Balancing the response to prescription drug abuse: Report of a national symposium on medicine and public policy* (pp. 109-117). Chicago: American Medical Association, Department of Substance Abuse.

DuPont, R.L. (1990d). A practical approach to benzodiazepine discontinuation. *Journal of Psychiatric Research, 24*(Suppl. 2), 81-90.

DuPont, R.L. (1990e). Thinking about stopping treatment for panic disorder. *Journal of Clinical Psychiatry, 51*(12, Suppl. A), 38-45.

DuPont, R.L. (1992a). Advances in the treatment of anxiety disorders: Part I. Psychological treatments. *Directions in Psychiatry, 12*(Lesson 24), 1-8. New York: Hatherleigh Co., Ltd.

DuPont, R.L. (1992b). Advances in the treatment of anxiety disorders: Part II. Pharmacological treatments. *Directions in Psychiatry, 12*(Lesson 25), 1-8. New York: Hatherleigh Co., Ltd.

DuPont, R.L. (1992c). Choosing the right treatment for the patient with anxiety. *Modern Medicine, 60*, 64-76.

DuPont, R.L. (1994). The twelve step approach. In N.S. Miller (Ed.), *Treating coexisting psychiatric and addictive disorders* (pp. 177-197). Center City, MN: Hazelden Educational Materials.

DuPont, R.L., & Baumgartner, W.A. (1995). Drug testing by urine and hair analysis: Complementary features and scientific issues. *Forensic Science International, 70*, 63-76.

DuPont, R.L., & DuPont, C.M. (1994). The treatment of anxiety: Realistic expectations and risks posed by controlled substances. *Journal of Law, Medicine & Ethics, 22*, 5-13.

DuPont, R.L., & Saylor, K.E. (1991). Sedatives/hypnotics and benzodiazepines. In R.J. Frances & S.I. Miller (Eds.), *Clinical textbook of addictive disorders* (pp. 69-102). New York: Guilford.

DuPont, R.L., & Saylor, K.E. (1992). Advances in the treatment of anxiety disorders: A therapist's guide. *Directions in Rehabilitation Counseling, 3*(Lesson 4), 1-27. New York: Hatherleigh Co., Ltd.

DuPont, R.L., Swinson, R.P., Ballenger, J.C., Burrows, G.D., Noyes, R., Rubin, R.T., Rifkin, A., & Pecknold, J.C. (1992). Discontinuation of alprazolam after long-term treatment of panic-related disorders. *Journal of Clinical Psychopharmacology, 12*, 352-354.

Ewing, J.A. (1984). Detecting alcoholism. The CAGE questionnaire. *Journal of the American Medical Association, 252*, 1905-1907.

Foderaro, L.W. (1995, February 19). Battling demons, and nicotine. *New York Times* (Metro Report Section), pp. 41, 48.

Frances, R.J., & Borg, L. (1993). The treatment of anxiety in patients with alcoholism. *Journal of Clinical Psychiatry, 54*(5, Suppl.), 37-43.

Hill, C.S. (1990). Clinical issues: Achieving balance in national drug control policy: The use of analgesia. In B.B. Wilford (Ed.), *Balancing the response to prescription drug abuse: Report of a national symposium on medicine and public policy* (pp. 37-48). Chicago: American Medical Association, Department of Substance Abuse.

Kaplan, H.I., Sadock, B.J., & Grebb, J.A. (1994). *Kaplan and Sadock's synopsis of psychiatry: Behavioral sciences, clinical psychiatry* (7th ed.). Baltimore: Williams & Wilkins.

Kessler, R.C., Edlund, M.J., Frank, R.G., Kendler, K.S., Leaf, P.J., Nelson, C.B., & Wittchen, H.-U. (1995). *Comorbidity of DSM-III-R mental disorders and substance disorders in the National Comorbidity Survey.* Manuscript submitted for publication.

Kessler, R.C., McGonagle, K.A., Zhao, S., Nelson, C.B., Hughes, M., Eshleman, S., Wittchen, H.-U., & Kendler, K.S. (1994). Lifetime and 12-month prevalence of DSM-III-R psychiatric disorders in the United States: Results from the National Comorbidity Survey. *Archives of General Psychiatry, 51*, 8-19.

Kessler, R.C., Nelson, C.B., McGonagle, K.A., Edlund, M.J., Frank, R.G., & Leaf, P.J. (in press). The epidemiology of co-occurring mental disorders and substance use disorders in the National Comorbidity Survey: Implications for prevention and service utilization. *American Journal of Orthopsychiatry.*

Kushner, M.G., Sher, K.J., & Beitman, B.D. (1990). The relation between alcohol problems and the anxiety disorders. *American Journal of Psychiatry,* 147, 685-695.

Lader, M. (1990). Benzodiazepine withdrawal. In R. Noyes, M. Roth, & G.D. Burrows (Eds.), *Handbook of anxiety: Vol. 4. The treatment of anxiety* (pp. 57-71). Amsterdam, The Netherlands: Elsevier.

Linnoila, M.I. (1989). Anxiety and alcoholism. *Journal of Clinical Psychiatry,* 50(11, Suppl.), 26-29.

Miller, N.S. (Ed.). (1994). Comorbid psychiatric and addiction disorders. *Psychiatric Annals,* 24(8).

Morrissey, E.R., & Schuckit, M.A. (1978). Stressful life events and alcohol problems among women seen at a detoxification center. *Journal of Studies on Alcohol,* 39, 1559-1576.

Nunes, E.V., McGrath, P.J., & Quitkin, F.M. (1995). Treating anxiety in patients with alcoholism. *Journal of Clinical Psychiatry,* 56(Suppl. 2), 3-9.

Regier, D.A., Farmer, M.E., Rae, D.S., Locke, B.Z., Keith, S.J., Judd, L.L., & Goodwin, F.K. (1990). Comorbidity of mental disorders with alcohol and other drug abuse. *Journal of the American Medical Association,* 264, 2511-2518.

Robins, L.N., & Regier, D.A. (Eds.). (1991). *Psychiatric disorders in America: The Epidemiologic Catchment Area study.* New York: Free Press.

Ross, J. (1994). *Triumph over fear: A book of help and hope for people with anxiety, panic attacks, and phobias.* New York: Bantam Books.

Roth, M. (1989). Anxiety disorders and the use and abuse of drugs. *Journal of Clinical Psychiatry,* 50(11, Suppl.), 30-35.

Saylor, K.E., DuPont, R.L., & Brouillard, M. (1990). Self-help treatment of anxiety disorders. In R. Noyes, M. Roth, & G.D. Burrows (Eds.), *Handbook of anxiety: Vol. 4. The treatment of anxiety* (pp. 483-496). Amsterdam, The Netherlands: Elsevier.

Schuckit, M.A. (1994). Low level of response to alcohol as a predictor of future alcoholism. *American Journal of Psychiatry,* 151, 184-189.

Schuckit, M.A., & Hesselbrock, V. (1994). Alcohol dependence and anxiety disorders: What is the relationship? *American Journal of Psychiatry,* 151, 1723-1734.

Sellers, E.M., Ciraulo, D.A., DuPont, R.L., Griffiths, R.R., Kosten, T.R., Romach, M.K., & Woody, G.E. (1993). Alprazolam and benzodiazepine dependence. *Journal of Clinical Psychiatry,* 54(10, Suppl.), 64-77.

U.S. Department of Health and Human Services. (1988a). Mandatory guidelines for federal workplace drug testing programs. *Federal Register* (April 11, 1988), pp. 11979-11989.

U.S. Department of Health and Human Services. (1988b). *Medical Review Officer manual: A guide to evaluating urine drug analysis* (DHHS Publication No. [ADM]88-1526). Washington, DC: U.S. Government Printing Office.

Weissman, M.M. (1988). Anxiety and alcoholism. *Journal of Clinical Psychiatry,* 49(10, Suppl.), 17-19.

Wilford, B.B. (Ed.). (1990). *Balancing the response to prescription drug abuse: Report of a national symposium on medicine and public policy.* Chicago: American Medical Association, Department of Substance Abuse.

5. Anxiety Disorders in Primary Care

M. Katherine Shear, MD
Herbert C. Schulberg, PhD

Recent epidemiological studies identify anxiety disorders as the most prevalent psychiatric disorders in the community (Kessler et al., 1994; Regier, Goldberg, & Taube, 1978). These studies also indicate that individuals with anxiety disorders present for treatment at general medical facilities as often as they present to specialty mental health providers (Regier et al., 1993). However, it is clear that primary care providers do not recognize and treat effectively individuals suffering from anxiety disorders, possibly because of different presentation of these disorders in the general health setting.

Valid and reliable diagnostic procedures and efficacious treatment strategies for anxiety disorders have been developed in psychiatric settings over the past two decades. However, application of these diagnostic and treatment methods has not been well studied in primary care settings, where there is some indication that both presentation of illness and effective treatment interventions may differ from those in the specialized psychiatric setting. On the other hand, recent work by Schulberg, Madonia et al. (1995) suggests that major depression in many primary care patients does not differ in severity or in treatment responsiveness from major depression experienced by patients who present to psychiatric settings. Thus there is a need to facilitate dissemination of efficacious methodologies to primary care settings. To do so, similarities and differences between primary care patients and psychiatric patients must be identified, and treatments must be tested in primary care settings. The purpose of this paper is to provide an overview of recent research on anxiety disorders in primary care. We will review: (1) prevalence of anxiety in the community and in primary care patients, (2) presentation of anxiety disorders in primary care, (3) recognition of anxiety and depression by primary care physicians, and (4) treatments that might be feasible and useful in primary care.

Prevalence of anxiety in primary care patients

The 1978 report by the President's Commission on Mental Health stressed the need for improved measures of prevalence and care of mental disorders, resulting in initiation of the NIMH-sponsored

Dr. Shear is an associate professor of psychiatry in the Department of Psychiatry at the University of Pittsburgh School of Medicine, where Dr. Schulberg is a professor of psychiatry, psychology, and medicine. Dr. Shear is also director of the Anxiety Disorders Program at Western Psychiatric Institute and Clinic, Pittsburgh, Pennsylvania, where Dr. Schulberg is director of the Primary Care Consultation Program.

Epidemiologic Catchment Area (ECA) Program to assess the prevalence of psychiatric disorders and the use of health care in different care-giving sectors. According to the ECA findings, the estimated one-year prevalence of anxiety disorders was 13%, approximately 20 million persons. Phobias had a one-year prevalence rate of 11% (about 17 million people). For panic disorder, the rate was 1% (2 million persons), while the rate for obsessive-compulsive disorder (OCD) was 2% (3 million persons). In addition, the ECA study yielded overall estimates of the number of individuals receiving treatment for these disorders in the general medical system. About 6 million persons received treatment for anxiety disorders, 5 million for phobias, 1 million for panic disorder, and 1.5 million for OCD (Regier et al., 1993).

In one year, 35.1 million people were affected by a psychiatric disorder, 20 million of whom (12.6%) suffered from an anxiety disorder. Chronicity of anxiety disorders was estimated to be higher than addictive disorders, lower than schizophrenia, and about the same as affective disorders. General medical physicians provided mental and addictive disorder treatment services to 6.4% of the population (10,043,000 persons per year). Twenty-three million people (14.7% of the adult population) sought mental health treatment in some sector, either general medical, specialty mental health, health services, or voluntary support network. Overall, the 6.4 million people with anxiety disorders who received treatment made 98 million visits (i.e., 15.4 visits per person per year). Of these persons, 87% were seen in professional settings. General medical practitioners saw 46% of them (12% of the visits). More than 1% of the anxiety disorder visits were to hospital emergency rooms.

Other studies address questions about the prevalence of anxiety disorders in primary care. Fifer et al. (1994) were interested in the rate of untreated anxiety in patients involved in prepaid health maintenance organizations. They found that 33% of 6,307 waiting-room respondents met screen criteria. By self-report, 44% of the patients had been recognized and treated for anxiety, while 56% had not. Fifer et al. did additional study of 647 untreated screen-positive patients. They found that 52% of the patients met criteria for one or more anxiety disorder diagnoses; 28% met criteria for multiple diagnoses. In addition, the prevalence of specific anxiety disorders among these untreated screen-positive patients was: posttraumatic stress disorder, 17%; simple phobia, 15%; social phobia, 14%; agoraphobia, 13%; generalized anxiety disorder, 9%; panic disorder, 5%; and obsessions, 4%. Patients with symptoms of anxiety had significant impairment in functioning and well-being whether or not they met criteria for a *DSM-III-R* diagnosis.

We recently assessed 330 patients at four primary care centers in Pittsburgh (Shear, Schulberg, & Madonia, 1994) using a structured diagnostic interview (the Primary Care Evaluation of Mental Disorders [PRIME-MD]; Spitzer et al., 1994) and found prevalence rates of 11% for panic disorder and 10% for generalized anxiety disorder. Similar to those in the Fifer et al. (1994) study, patients who met criteria for panic disorder, generalized anxiety disorder, or both had: (1) high rates of comorbidity with depression and other anxiety disorders, (2) significant impairment in functioning as measured by the Medical Outcomes Study Short-Form 36 (MOS SF-36; Ware & Sherbourne, 1992), and (3) a high rate of referral for mental health consultation.

Comorbidity with depression is common in anxiety disorders, and patients who endorse both mood and anxiety symptoms may be particularly prevalent in primary care. There is some evidence that a majority of patients presenting to primary care settings have comorbid anxiety and depressive symptoms. Schulberg, Block, and Madonia (1995) found that 75% of a group of patients who met criteria for current major depression had a lifetime history of comorbid anxiety disorder, and Shear et al. (1994) found that 80% of patients who met criteria for current panic disorder or generalized anxiety disorder also reported lifetime major depression. Fifer et al. (1994) reported a similar 70% rate of elevated symptoms of depression in patients with untreated anxiety. An important group of patients in primary care suffers from a newly defined syndrome called "mixed anxiety-depression" (Katon & Roy-Byrne, 1991; Zinbarg et al., 1994). These patients have distressing and debilitating mood and anxiety symptoms but fail to meet full diagnostic criteria for either an anxiety or a depressive disorder. Repeated studies of psychological symptoms in primary care patients have found this constellation to be prevalent, leading to consideration of a new diagnostic category in *DSM-IV*. However, the decision of the work group was to add mixed anxiety-depression to the nomenclature only in the form of an appendix, although it is included in the body of *ICD-10* (Wittchen & Essau, 1993).

To meet the proposed *DSM-IV* diagnostic criteria for mixed anxiety-depression, a person would have to experience persistent or recurrent dysphoria for at least one month, along with at least four of the following symptoms: difficulty concentrating, disturbed sleep, fatigue, irritability, worry, crying easily, hypervigilance, expecting the worst, a sense of hopelessness, and low self-esteem or feelings of worthlessness. These symptoms must cause clinically recognizable impairment in the person's life, including in social and work activities, and they are not the result of a general medical condition or of a drug (either medication or a drug of abuse). In addition, the person has not met and does not currently meet criteria for another anxiety or mood disorder, and his or her symptoms are not better explained by the existence of another psychiatric disorder (American Psychiatric Association, 1994, pp. 724-725).

A field trial of mixed anxiety-depression identified prevalence rates of 6.6% in primary care settings and 11.7% in psychiatric anxiety disorder clinics (Zinbarg et al., 1994). In Fifer et al.'s (1994) study, 26% of the screen-positive group had anxiety and depressive symptoms that failed to meet full diagnostic criteria, compared to 30% who met criteria for an anxiety disorder alone and 43% who met criteria for comorbid anxiety and depression. Studies confirm the increased distress and impairment and increased health care utilization rates in the mixed anxiety-depression group. For example, when Fifer et al. compared levels of distress and impairment in the three groups, they found mixed anxiety-depression to be associated with more impairment than with anxiety disorders alone and somewhat less than with comorbid anxiety and depressive disorders.

Subsyndromal anxiety without depression is also prevalent and associated with impairment. Symptoms of anxiety occur commonly in reaction to life stress, but they are more severe and debilitating in some individuals than in others. In most studies, subjects with subclinical anxiety symptoms, such as infrequent panic attacks, are found to be significantly more symptomatic on other measures of anxiety and depression than are nonsymptomatic controls. Thus there is good reason to identify and treat these individuals, whose treatments may be brief and primarily psychosocial.

Presentation of anxiety disorders in primary care

Of all patients in primary care, 25-40% have no medical diagnosis, and 30-60% of their visits are for symptoms lacking an underlying physical disorder (Vásquez-Barquero, Wilkinson, Williams, Diez-Manrique, & Peña, 1990). Patients with no medical diagnosis do, however, have a high prevalence of psychiatric illness. Anxiety and depression are associated with a range of somatic symptoms, which sometimes become the focus of the patient's concern and motivate a visit to a general practitioner. Van Hemert, Hengeveld, Bolk, Rooijmans, and Vandenbroucke (1993) evaluated psychiatric disorders in 191 newly referred patients in a general medical clinic. They found psychiatric disorders more prevalent in patients whose symptoms were not well explained by physical illness. The rate of psychiatric disorders was 15% when symptoms were well explained, compared to 38-45% when symptoms were ill-explained or unex-plained by physical illness. Presenting complaints in 30% of patients with no medical illness included fatigue, gastrointestinal symptoms, dizziness, joint pain, weight loss, chest pain, and headache. Thirty-eight percent of those with unexplained symptoms were found to have a diagnosable psychiatric disorder, including 19% with depres-sive neurosis and 12% with anxiety or phobic neurosis. Among patients with doubtful medical illness, depression was diagnosed in 33% and anxiety in 12%. Studies of patients with atypical chest pain reveal a very high percentage who meet criteria for panic disorder (up to 83% in some studies). Unrecognized and untreated, these patients typically wander from physician to physician. In fact, Sheehan (1982) reported that the average patient consulted 10 different physicians before coming to an anxiety disorder clinic.

Other studies confirm the high prevalence of anxiety and depres-sive disorders in patients who come for treatment of fatigue and in those diagnosed with chronic fatigue syndrome. Kruesi, Dale, and Straus (1989) found that 75% of such patients had a psychiatric dis-order, usually predating the onset of the chronic fatigue. In addition, 40% met criteria for an anxiety disorder. Other common somatic complaints are also frequent in patients with anxiety disorders. In a review of common symptoms associated with anxiety disorders, Sharpe, Peveler, and Mayou (1992) found atypical chest pain, palpi-tations, breathlessness, abdominal pain, dizziness, and syncope.

In Katon's (1984) study of 55 panic disorder patients referred for psychiatric consultation by primary care physicians, 89% had pre-sented with one or two somatic complaints, which had been mis-diagnosed for months or years. Cardiac, gastrointestinal, and neurological symptoms were most common. Clancy and Noyes (1976) found that 30 categories of tests had been performed on 71 patients with anxiety neurosis, including a total of 358 tests and pro-cedures (range 0-11, mean 7.5) and 135 specialty consultations. Other studies have documented high levels of anxiety and depression in patients presenting with chest pain and normal coronary arteries (Costa et al., 1985; Elias, Robbins, Blow, Rice, & Edgecomb, 1982). Ford (1987) found that, compared to controls without chest pain, patients in the ECA study with chest pain were four times as likely to have panic disorder, three times as likely to have phobic disorder, and twice as likely to have depression.

Anxiety disorders are also comorbid with medical disorders. Irri-table bowel patients have elevated rates of panic disorder (Drossman et al., 1988; Lydiard, Laraia, Howell, & Ballenger, 1986). Anxiety and/or depression in patients with a chronic medical illness can am-

75

plify the symptoms of the medical illness (Bridges & Goldberg, 1985), probably because of increased reporting of symptoms, heightened attention to bodily sensations, and/or somatic consequences of increased physiological arousal.

Rogers et al. (1994) reported on patients evaluated in the Harvard-Brown long-term naturalistic follow-up project (HARP) and examined the relationship between physical illness and anxiety from another perspective. These researchers reported high levels of medical illness in a group of 711 anxiety disorder patients. Their findings emphasize the complexities of evaluating medical illness in individuals with anxiety disorders. Although anxiety may present with somatic symptoms, in the absence of a diagnosable medical condition, it is also possible that anxiety states are associated with a heightened prevalence of physical illness. Sympathetic arousal related to the anxiety disorder may provoke or maintain the physical illness. Real physical illness may also act to initiate or maintain an anxiety disorder. In either case, the Rogers et al. study highlights the fact that the presence of an anxiety disorder is not only a differential diagnostic issue in medical illness. Anxiety may also be found as a clinically significant comorbid condition. If medical comorbidity is untreated, it may prolong the anxiety disorder. Similarly, untreated anxiety disorders may prolong the course and worsen the outcome of medical illness.

It is possible that the presence of an anxiety disorder increases the risk for development of some medical disorders. For example, several studies have found an increased prevalence of hypertension in panic disorder patients. Katon (1986) found a 13.6% prevalence of hypertension in primary care patients diagnosed with panic, compared to 4.4% in controls without such a diagnosis.

Recognition of anxiety and depression by primary care physicians

Studies conducted in the United States and Europe document the fact that generalist physicians provide care for patients with psychological disorders more frequently than do mental health providers. Primary care providers are also likely to be the sole source of recognition and treatment of these disorders. Nevertheless, many primary care physicians lack the skills needed to diagnose and treat psychiatric disorders, even though most consider it their responsibility to manage psychiatric illness. Ormel and colleagues (1990) noted that more than one third of patients in general practice settings experience substantial levels of psychological distress, and up to 25% meet diagnostic criteria for a specific disorder, usually an anxiety or depressive disorder. Prevalence rates ranging from 15% to 46% were found for individuals with significant mental distress, depending on the type of screening instrument. In the study by Ormel et al., general practitioners failed to identify half the cases, with depression recognized more frequently than anxiety disorders. Detection was better for more severe symptoms, and recognition was strongly associated with management and outcome. Fifer et al. (1994) confirmed the high rate of unrecognized anxiety disorders in primary care. This work highlights the need for and value of improving recognition and management skills among primary care providers.

Broadhead (1994) discussed four factors that contribute to the difficulty of diagnosing mental disorders in primary care: (1) patients often present with a mix of psychological and somatic symptoms that are not part of established diagnostic criteria for mental disorder, (2) the presentation of some well-described mental disorders may be different in primary care, (3) a significant number of patients experience symptoms and impairment that fail to meet duration or severity criteria for mental disorder, and (4) patients from diverse cultural backgrounds may have different ways of expressing symptoms. With regard to the fourth factor, Broadhead drew attention to several culturally related syndromes. In Latin America and the southwestern United States, patients present as "asustados." "Sustos," which means fright, occurs in association with symptoms of anxiety, depression, and somatization. Specific symptoms include anorexia, weight loss, debility, night-time insomnia, daytime drowsiness, irritability, exaggerated startle reaction, diarrhea, spontaneous fainting, and hysterical episodes. Hispanics suffer from attacks of "nerves" in which they experience acute panic-like attacks, with a wave of tension that may be manifested by shaking and quivering of the body, stomach pains and nausea, headaches, heart tremors, shortness of breath, chest pain, dizziness, trembling in extremities, blurred vision, and hot flashes. This acute attack is followed by a state of lethargy, sadness, tension, insomnia, and feelings of weariness or obsessive worrying. Physical signs include heaviness in the chest, arms, and head. African-Americans are more likely to experience somatic symptoms without the psychological concomitants. A high prevalence of panic disorder and sleep paralysis has been reported in hypertensive African-Americans, compared to those without hypertension (Neal, Rich, & Smucker, 1994).

Improved recognition of anxiety and depression in primary care patients has been a subject of major concern because, as Ford (1994) pointed out, at least 50% of patients with mental disorders receive all or part of their care from general practitioners. About 5-20% of visits to these practitioners involve patients with ongoing mental disorders.

Recognition has been studied using the Identification Index, which measures the physician's ability to correctly identify probable psychiatric cases (Gask, 1992). Bias measures the tendency to overdiagnose or underdiagnose. In general, those who score high on the Identification Index have a tendency to overdiagnose. Patient, physician, and system variables influence detection (Ford, 1994), with females often being overdiagnosed. Older physicians and female physicians are more likely to make diagnoses. Physicians with more training and better overall knowledge are more likely to recognize psychiatric illness.

Studies of interview styles have identified those styles associated with eliciting or suppressing patient information. These observations have been used to develop recognition training programs, which have met with some success (Gask, 1992). Skills taught to physicians in these training programs include enhancing the ability to recognize and respond to verbal and nonverbal cues, asking about health beliefs, making empathic comments, and using patient-directed, open-ended interviewing strategies. Gask's (1992) work indicates that physicians trained in this way can reduce the anxiety of their patients. Physicians reported that the techniques were helpful and that they saved time as a result of their improved ability to recognize and manage emotional distress.

Treatment strategies for primary care providers

Most primary care physicians are not fully trained to treat psychiatric illness. Such training includes the administration of medication and the provision of psychotherapy. In Great Britain, efforts to provide psychotherapy training to general practitioners have had some success. In the United States, pharmaceutical company representatives often provide the information used by physicians to treat anxiety and depression in their patients. Nevertheless, Schulberg, Block, et al. (1995) have suggested that a physician's "usual care" of depression leads to a poor outcome. This finding raises questions about who should treat these patients. Clearly, training will be needed if general practitioners are to provide care for patients with psychiatric disorders. It is also possible that such treatment can be performed effectively by physician extenders, such as nurses, social workers, or physicians' assistants. It is likely, however, that a substantial minority of patients will be treatment-resistant and will require referral to specialty services.

There are now well-proven efficacious treatments for both anxiety and depression using medication and psychotherapy, alone and in combination. These treatments have not been well studied in primary care settings, and thus their effectiveness remains to be documented. However, there is no reason to expect that these efficacious interventions would not be useful in primary care. This conclusion is supported by Schulberg, Madonia, et al.'s (1995) study, which documents the effectiveness of medication and interpersonal psychotherapy in treating depression in the primary care setting.

Although standard psychiatric treatment may be the optimal approach to diagnosable syndromes in primary care, it may not always be practical. Moreover, Ormel et al. (1990) found that improvement in outcome was not related to mental health treatment. This finding raises the possibility that a more minimal intervention may be helpful to many patients in this setting. Several investigators have explored the usefulness of brief psychological treatments for primary care patients. Although this work is still unfinished, some early results are promising. For example, Milne, Jones, and Walters (1989) suggested that improving social supports by training informal providers (e.g., former clients) may be a cost-effective strategy for improving outcome. Barkham (1989) reported preliminary results from a three-session cognitive-behavioral intervention. In the first session, a problem is identified and a behavioral solution is planned, along with provision of some cognitive strategies for managing the problematic situation. In the second session a week later, the behavioral exercise is discussed and further cognitive work is done. The third session, 3 months later, consists of a review of the usefulness of the new strategies and an assessment of symptoms. A third approach, suggested by White and Keenan (1990), is for a large-group didactic "course" on anxiety management strategies.

Other researchers have suggested brief problem-solving therapy, which has been as effective as benzodiazepine treatment of anxiety disorder patients (Mynors-Wallis & Gath, 1992). Finally, Swinson, Soulios, Cox, and Kuch (1992) showed that panic disorder patients provided with psychoeducation and exposure instructions in an emergency room setting had a significantly better outcome than those not so informed. These innovative, brief approaches show considerable promise as first-line interventions for large groups of anxiety disorder patients seen in general medical settings. However, as Ormel and colleagues (1990) have found, more severely ill patients have a more pessimistic outlook and will undoubtedly require the more sophisticated and well-tested interventions currently being advocated for psychiatric patients.

For anxiety disorders, cognitive-behavioral strategies have been developed that are specific for each disorder. Disorder-specific efficacious medications have also been identified and tested. In particular, tricyclic antidepressants and selective serotonin reuptake inhibitors are effective for treating panic disorder, while azaspirones and tricyclic antidepressants are efficacious for generalized anxiety disorder. It is not our purpose in this paper to review these interventions in detail, but the interested reader can consult one of the several texts available on this topic (Ballenger, 1986; Fyer & Sandberg, 1988; Montgomery, Bullock, & Fineberg, 1991; Pollack & Rosenbaum, 1988; Roy-Byrne, Wingerson, Cowley, & Dager, 1993).

Finally, a caveat is needed when discussing proven efficacious treatments, because studies of long-term outcome of these treatments have not yet been conducted. However, substantial evidence exists to support the likelihood that anxiety disorders are chronic recurrent illnesses, with high levels of comorbidity with depression. Consequently, once identified, a patient with an anxiety disorder should be assessed for anxiety and depressive symptomatology at each primary care visit. Early counseling intervention with such patients, use of maintenance medication, or a combination of counseling and medication may provide important symptom relief. Improvement in anxiety symptomatology is expected to lead to fewer problems with somatic symptoms, fewer health care visits, less functional impairment, and improved quality of life.

References

American Psychiatric Association. (1994). *Diagnostic and statistical manual of mental disorders* (4th ed.). Washington, DC: Author.

Ballenger, J.C. (1986). Pharmacotherapy of the panic disorders. *Journal of Clinical Psychiatry, 47*(6, Suppl.), 27-32.

Barkham, M. (1989). Brief prescriptive therapy in two-plus-one sessions: Initial cases from the clinic. *Behavioural Psychotherapy, 17,* 161-175.

Bridges, K.W., & Goldberg, D.P. (1985). Somatic presentation of DSM-III psychiatric disorder in primary care. *Journal of Psychosomatic Research, 29,* 563-569.

Broadhead, W.E. (1994). Presentation of psychiatric symptomatology in primary care. In J. Miranda, A.A. Hohmann, C.C. Attkisson, & D.B. Larson (Eds.), *Mental disorders in primary care* (pp. 139-162). San Francisco: Jossey-Bass.

Clancy, J., & Noyes, R., Jr. (1976). Anxiety neurosis: A disease for the medical model. *Psychosomatics, 17,* 90-93.

Costa, P.T., Zonderman, A.B., Engel, B.T., Baile, W.F., Brimlow, D.L., & Brinker, J. (1985). The relation of chest pain symptoms to angiographic findings of coronary artery stenosis and neuroticism. *Psychosomatic Medicine, 47,* 285-293.

Drossman, D.A., McKee, D.C., Sandler, R.S., Mitchell, C.M., Cramer, E.M., Lowman, B.C., & Berger, A.L. (1988). Psychosocial factors in the irritable bowel syndrome: A multivariate study of patients and nonpatients with irritable bowel syndrome. *Gastroenterology, 95,* 701-708.

Elias, M.F., Robbins, M.A., Blow, F.C., Rice, A.P., & Edgecomb, J.L. (1982). Symptom reporting, anxiety and depression in arteriographically classified middle-aged chest pain patients. *Experimental Aging Research, 8,* 45-51.

Fifer, S.K., Mathias, S.D., Patrick, D.L., Mazonson, P.D., Lubeck, D.P., & Buesching, D.P. (1994). Untreated anxiety among adult primary care patients in a health maintenance organization. *Archives of General Psychiatry, 51,* 740-750.

Ford, D. (1987). *The relationship of psychiatric illness to medically unexplained chest pain.* Paper presented at Mental Disorders in General Health Care Settings, a Research Conference, Seattle, WA.

Ford, D.E. (1994). Recognition and under-recognition of mental disorders in adult primary care. In J. Miranda, A.A. Hohmann, C.C. Attkisson, & D.B. Larson (Eds.), *Mental disorders in primary care* (pp. 186-205). San Francisco: Jossey-Bass.

Fyer, A.J., & Sandberg, D. (1988). Pharmacologic treatment of panic disorder. In A.J. Frances & R.E. Hales (Eds.), *American Psychiatric Press review of psychiatry* (Vol. 7, pp. 88-120). Washington, DC: American Psychiatric Press.

Gask, L. (1992). Training general practitioners to detect and manage emotional disorders. *International Review of Psychiatry 4,* 293-300.

Katon, W. (1984). Panic disorder and somatization: Review of 55 cases. *American Journal of Medicine, 77,* 101-106.

Katon, W. (1986). Panic disorder: Epidemiology, diagnosis, and treatment in primary care. *Journal of Clinical Psychiatry, 47*(10, Suppl.), 21-27.

Katon, W., & Roy-Byrne, P.P. (1991). Mixed anxiety and depression. *Journal of Abnormal Psychology, 100,* 337-345.

Kessler, R.C., McGonagle, K.A., Zhao, S., Nelson, C.B., Hughes, M., Eshleman, S., Wittchen, H.-U., & Kendler, K.S. (1994). Lifetime and 12-month prevalence of DSM-III-R psychiatric disorders in the United States: Results from the National Comorbidity Study. *Archives of General Psychiatry, 51,* 8-19.

Kruesi, M.J., Dale, J., & Straus, S.E. (1989). Psychiatric diagnoses in patients who have chronic fatigue syndrome. *Journal of Clinical Psychiatry, 50,* 53-56.

Lydiard, R.B., Laraia, M.T., Howell, E.F., & Ballenger, J.C. (1986). Can panic disorder present as irritable bowel syndrome? *Journal of Clinical Psychiatry, 47,* 470-473.

Milne, D.L., Jones, R.Q., & Walters, P. (1989). Anxiety management in the community: A social support model and preliminary evaluation. *Behavioural Psychotherapy, 17,* 221-226.

Montgomery, S.A., Bullock, T., & Fineberg, N. (1991). Serotonin selectivity for obsessive compulsive and panic disorders. *Journal of Psychiatry and Neuroscience, 16*(2, Suppl. 1), 30-35.

Mynors-Wallis, L.M., & Gath, D.H. (1992). Brief psychological treatments. *International Review of Psychiatry, 4,* 301-305.

Neal, A.M., Rich, L.N., & Smucker, D. (1994). The presence of panic disorder among African American hypertensives: A pilot study. *Journal of Black Psychology, 20,* 29-35.

Ormel, J., Van den Brink, W., Koeter, M.W.J., Giel, R., Van der Meer, K., Van de Willige, G., & Wilmink, F.W. (1990). Recognition, management and outcome of psychological disorders in primary care: A naturalistic follow-up study. *Psychological Medicine, 20,* 909-923.

Pollack, M.H., & Rosenbaum, J.F. (1988). Benzodiazepines in panic-related disorders. *Journal of Anxiety Disorders, 2,* 95-107.

Regier, D.A., Goldberg, I.D., & Taube, C.A. (1978). The de facto U.S. mental health services system: A public health perspective. *Archives of General Psychiatry, 35,* 685-693.

Regier, D.A., Narrow, W.E., Rae, D.S., Mandersheid, R.W., Locke, B.Z., & Goodwin, F.K. (1993). The de facto U.S. mental and addictive disorders service system. *Archives of General Psychiatry, 50,* 85-94.

Rogers, M.P., White, K., Warshaw, M.G., Yonkers, K.A., Rodriguez-Villa, F., Chang, G., & Keller, M.B. (1994). Prevalence of medical illness in patients with anxiety disorders. *International Journal of Psychiatry in Medicine, 24,* 83-96.

Roy-Byrne, P., Wingerson, D., Cowley, D., & Dager, S. (1993). Psychopharmacologic treatment of panic, generalized anxiety disorder and social phobia. *Psychiatric Clinics of North America, 16,* 719-735.

Schulberg, H.C., Block, M., & Madonia, M. (1995). *Treating major depression in primary care practice: Eight-month clinical outcomes.* Manuscript submitted for publication.

Schulberg, H.C., Madonia, M.J., Block, M.R., Coulehan, J.L., Scott, C.P., Rodriguez, E., & Black, A. (1995). Major depression in primary care practice: Clinical characteristics and treatment implications. *Psychosomatics, 36,* 129-137.

Sharpe, M., Peveler, R., & Mayou, R. (1992). The psychological treatment of patients with functional somatic symptoms: A practical guide. *Journal of Psychosomatic Research, 36,* 515-529.

Shear, M.K., Schulberg, H.C., & Madonia, M. (1994, September). *Panic and generalized anxiety disorder in primary care.* Paper presented at a meeting of the Association for Primary Care, Washington, DC.

Sheehan, D.V. (1982). Current concepts in psychiatry: Panic attacks and phobias. *New England Journal of Medicine, 307,* 156-158.

Spitzer, R.L., Williams, J.B.W., Kroenke, K., Linzer, M., deGruy III, F.V., Hahn, S.R., Brody, D., & Johnson, J.G. (1994). Utility of a new procedure for diagnosing mental disorder in primary care: The PRIME-MD 1000 Study. *Journal of the American Medical Association, 272,* 1749-1756.

Swinson, R.P., Soulios, C., Cox, B.J., & Kuch, K. (1992). Brief treatment of emergency room patients with panic attacks. *American Journal of Psychiatry, 149,* 944-946.

Van Hemert, A.M., Hengeveld, M.W., Bolk, J.H., Rooijmans, H.G.M., & Vandenbroucke, J.P. (1993). Psychiatric disorders in relation to medical illness among patients of a general medical out-patient clinic. *Psychological Medicine, 23,* 167-173.

Vásquez-Barquero, J.L., Wilkinson, G., Williams, P., Diez-Manrique, J.F., & Peña, C. (1990). Mental health and medical consultation in primary care settings. *Psychological Medicine, 20,* 681-694.

Ware J.E., Jr., & Sherbourne, C.D. (1992). The MOS 36-item short-form health survey (SF-36): I. Conceptual framework and item selection. *Medical Care, 30,* 473-483.

White, J., & Keenan, M. (1990). Stress control: A pilot study of large group therapy for generalized anxiety disorder. *Behavioural Psychotherapy, 18,* 143-146.

Wittchen, H.-U., & Essau, C.A. (1993). Comorbidity and mixed anxiety-depressive disorders: Is there epidemiologic evidence? *Journal of Clinical Psychiatry, 54*(Suppl. 1), 9-15.

Zinbarg, R.E., Barlow, D.H., Liebowitz, M., Street, L., Broadhead, E., Katon, W., Roy-Byrne, P., Lepine, J.-P., Teherani, M., Richards, J., Brantley, P.J., & Kraemer, H. (1994). The DSM-IV field trial for mixed anxiety-depression. *American Journal of Psychiatry, 151,* 1153-1162.

6. Challenges to Providing Integrated Treatment of Anxiety Disorders

W. Walter Menninger, MD

Anxiety is a basic, ubiquitous emotional experience. Its discomforting, unsettling feelings provoke the individual to seek relief, either by mastery or by avoidance and escape from the anxiety-provoking situation. With a lifetime prevalence of nearly 15% and a one-month prevalence of 7.3%, diagnosable anxiety disorders are among the most common of emotional disorders (Regier, Narrow, & Rae, 1990). In view of this prevalence, one might assume that all practitioners would be familiar with and well versed in the diagnosis and treatment of these conditions. But such is not the case. Not only do primary care physicians fail to diagnose the conditions half the time (Ormel et al., 1990; Shear & Schulberg, 1995), but they also frequently have not had the training or familiarity with psychotherapeutic and psychopharmacological treatments for anxiety. Similarly, psychiatrists are challenged to be alert to diagnosing these conditions and to keep up with new developments in understanding and treating them. Indeed, a considerable number of factors in today's health care scene contribute to the challenges to providing integrated treatment of anxiety disorders.

Challenge #1: Many patients suffering from anxiety disorders do not go to a psychiatrist for help.

The prevalence data from the Epidemiologic Catchment Area (ECA) study are not matched by the number of patients with anxiety disorders seeking help for that condition from psychiatrists. A great many patients, prompted by the somatic symptoms, seek help from primary care physicians, but the anxiety disorder is not diagnosed. Others are ashamed or fearful of the stigma associated with a "mental" or emotional illness and are discouraged from seeking help. One colleague (Beitman, 1995) reported the case of a middle-aged health care worker whose first panic attack occurred during adolescence. Her family physician assured her that there was "nothing wrong" physically. Told by her parents that she shouldn't talk to anyone about these attacks, she suffered with them for more than 20 years, living a constricted life. She sought help only when she saw an announcement

---

Dr. Menninger is president and chief executive officer of The Menninger Clinic, Topeka, Kansas.

of a research study on treatment of panic disorder in the hospital where she worked. A history of quiet desperation and limited hope for relief is not uncommon among patients with partially disabling anxiety disorders.

Challenge #2: When the patient with an anxiety disorder goes to the primary care physician, the condition may not be diagnosed and treated as such.

As noted, often the patient's physical symptoms prompt a visit with an internist or a general physician. However, the medical training of physicians orients them to focus on relieving somatic symptoms, and primary care physicians are not accustomed to routine exploration of psychiatric problems (Borus, Howes, Devins, Rosenberg, & Livingston, 1988). Furthermore, the patient may fail to report emotional distress to the physician (Eisenberg, 1992). After undergoing various examinations, and often after being referred for further studies by a variety of clinical specialists, the patient is advised, like the patient described earlier, "There is nothing wrong with you."

Challenge #3: Apparent differences in the prevalence of anxiety disorders in men and women and lack of careful gender-based research increase the complexity of diagnosis and treatment for both genders.

Current research findings indicate that anxiety disorders are about three times as common in women as in men. But as Zerbe (1995) has pointed out, "gender-based research is in its infancy" (p. 38). Thus, as research findings accumulate based on careful delineation of gender factors, including medical issues, the reproductive cycle, trauma (such as abuse), and marriage and the family, approaches to treatment are likely to be revised. In particular, treatment may become more individualized, not only for women but also for men.

Challenge #4: The comorbidity of anxiety disorders with depression and addiction complicates the formulation and execution of a treatment plan for these patients.

There is a high rate of comorbidity between depression and anxiety disorders, particularly panic disorder (Rosenbaum & Pollock, 1994). Similarly, DuPont (1995) has outlined the overlap of anxiety disorders and addiction. The treatment of patients with more than one clinical diagnosis requires special strategies. Such cases need a systematic clinical assessment to identify and differentiate the coexisting illnesses and a treatment plan that addresses each disorder. In persons with coexisting illness, the course of treatment is likely to be more complicated and lengthy, and the outcome less favorable. As DuPont noted, one approach does not fit all patients, and the use of certain medications with addicted patients must be carefully monitored.

Challenge #5: The multiplicity of presumed etiologies and ideologies may leave the physician and psychiatrist confused as to the best therapeutic plan to implement.

Rosenbaum, Pollock, Otto, and Pollack (1995) have reviewed at some length the etiological understanding of panic disorder, identifying biological and social learning theories for the basis of this disorder. One view is that panic disorder is a chronic condition related to a constitutional vulnerability involving dysregulation of the physiological system, while a second view is that panic disorder is related to the development of a "fear of fear." As such, the condition requires ongoing and perhaps lifelong medication. Yet practitioners who focus on the social learning perspective report that a cognitive-behavioral approach can be successful in achieving lasting symptom relief in a high percentage of cases (Barlow, 1992).

The evolution of competing ideologies in the psychiatric field—biological, psychodynamic, interpersonal, and behavioral—has also presented a challenge. As Klerman (1991) has noted, "Review of the role of ideology in relation to psychopharmacology and psychotherapy over the past three decades indicates a shift from preoccupations with theoretical preconceptions to attempts to deal with the growing demand for evidence" (p. 18). Controlled studies that assess the efficacy of so many variables are extraordinarily difficult to carry out. Yet, opined Klerman, "the availability of evidence for efficacy of combined therapies in various conditions will lead to cautious attempts at integration of theory and practice" (p. 18).

Challenge #6: The increase in the pharmacopoeia for the treatment of anxiety disorders threatens to outstrip the clinician's capacity to know what drug to use when and why.

Both Rosenbaum et al. (1995) and Marshall (1995) have reviewed the diverse antipanic and social phobia pharmacopoeia. The available medications range widely—tricyclic antidepressants, monoamine oxidase inhibitors, selective serotonin reuptake inhibitors, benzodiazepines, and beta-adrenergic blockers. Even the most sophisticated psychopharmacologically oriented psychiatrist must feel challenged in sorting out the wide range of dosages, drug interactions, side effects, and so forth. And the marketplace for new medications continues to burgeon as new applications are found for those substances originally released with a narrower focus of prescription.

Challenge #7: Untoward reactions to medications may not be simply idiosyncratic, but instead they may have significant meaning and consequential implications for the patient and the therapeutic outcome.

Beitman (1995), in the clinical case discussed earlier, noted an untoward drug reaction in a patient with a 24-year history of panic attacks. On a low-dose benzodiazepine, she experienced an increase in "energy" and a decrease in her panic attacks. But with a slight increase in the medication, she became hypomanic and then developed an acute paranoid reaction, feeling there was nobody in the world she could trust. She felt she needed to get a gun to protect herself, despite prior strong feelings against guns. These symptoms cleared when the dosage of the medication was reduced; and with some psychotherapeutic exploration, the patient gained insight regarding the experiences in her upbringing that prompted her lack of trust and fear of the world. Subsequently, the patient was able to separate more from her family of origin and to go places she had previously not been able to go. Thus what might have been viewed simply as an untoward drug reaction, when understood in the context of the patient's life and addressed psychotherapeutically, was indeed highly relevant in reducing the intensity and impact of the patient's anxiety disorder.

Challenge #8: Treatment may be complicated by the trend toward splitting psychiatric care into pharmacotherapy by the psychiatrist and psychotherapy by another mental health professional.

Chiles, Carlin, Benjamin, and Beitman (1991) reported the results of a survey in Washington State showing that nearly two thirds of the responding psychiatrists had seen at least one pharmacotherapy patient during the preceding month who was involved in psychotherapy with someone else. Chiles et al. found that such collaborative arrangements were common and usually worked well. But they noted, "The triangular relationship requires openness, trust, the ability to contact a colleague diplomatically on a puzzling treatment decision, and toleration for being questioned about one's own treatment decision" (p. 116). This "treatment triangle" does present questions regarding who is legally responsible for the patient and how confidentiality is dealt with. Communication is essential to assure the success of such divided therapeutic efforts.

Challenge #9: Limitations on access to and number of appointments for mental health care may restrict treatment options for patients with these disorders.

The opportunity to integrate pharmacotherapy and psychotherapy with these patients would preserve the clinician's option to explore the psychological ramifications of the medication's effect, when the patient is prepared to pursue them. Many health care plans, however, place significant limits on the number of clinical appointments (e.g., 8-10), so that the therapist and patient have to forgo such psychotherapeutic exploration.

Pressing for more cost-effective treatments, managed care has challenged clinicians to refer patients for group therapy and self-help group experiences. Another influence of managed care is the emphasis it places on limiting psychiatric participation to the prescription of medicine, with psychotherapy being provided by a master's-level psychologist or social worker. Beitman (in press) presents data, however, suggesting that 20-30 minutes of combined treatment by a psychiatrist could be less expensive than the divided treatment.

Discussion

The foregoing factors represent significant and ongoing challenges to providing effective, integrated treatment for patients with anxiety disorders—and for that matter, for patients with a wide range of other psychiatric disorders. Elsewhere, I (Menninger, 1992, 1994) have articulated eight principles of integrated treatment for anxiety disorders (see Table 1). These principles begin with an acknowledgment that anxiety in the patient can provoke anxiety in the therapist. Therefore it is important for the therapist to recognize and diagnose the anxiety disorder and potential comorbid conditions. The patient should be reassured that the symptoms are real. Commonly, symptomatic relief may be essential before psychological work can proceed. Furthermore, symptomatic relief may be facilitated by enhancing the patient's confidence about being able to control the symptoms. The patient needs to accept the condition as a psychiatric illness, and to cooperate with the therapist in a search to determine the underlying cause of the anxiety.

It is important to avoid the "either/or" view that these conditions are effectively treated by either a biological or a psychotherapeutic

Table 1. *Principles of integrated treatment for anxiety disorders*

1. *Anxiety in the patient can provoke anxiety in the therapist.*
   The urgency felt by the patient resonates with the physician's training to take remedial action to relieve discomfort and anguish.

2. *A careful differential diagnosis can help identify and address the problem of comorbidity.*
   Recognition of a secondary diagnostic issue may come only as the patient fails to respond effectively to treatment for the anxiety.

3. *The anxiety disorder is often not initially recognized as such.*
   Patients frequently seek help for physical symptoms from an internist or family practitioner who searches for a physical explanation for the problem.

4. *The patient should be reassured that the symptoms are real.*
   The patient may not feel the symptoms are valid or real if another physician has said "they're all in your head." The patient needs to be validated as having a known and diagnosable illness.

5. *The patient should be helped to accept the condition as a psychiatric illness.*
   Patients who can accept their illness as psychiatric will be more receptive to taking psychotropic medication. Otherwise, they may resist taking medication.

6. *Symptomatic relief may be essential before psychological work can proceed.*
   Effective treatment involves a two-stage approach, with medication to relieve acute anxiety, after which brief or open-ended psychotherapy and behavioral therapy may be used to facilitate the patient's capacity to deal with the anxiety and address the underlying problems.

7. *Symptomatic relief is facilitated by enhancing the patient's confidence about being able to remain in control.*
   Techniques to enhance an individual's sense of being in control diminish anxiety. Cognitive-behavioral approaches typically incorporate various methods of anxiety control, including distraction, coping self-statements, paradoxical intention, relaxation, and meditation.

8. *A search should be made to determine the underlying cause; until it is recognized, symptoms may persist.*
   A persistent and careful search usually enables the treater to identify a precipitating incident or conflict. If that is effectively addressed, the need for additional treatment or medication may be markedly reduced. Often, the patient may have a strong psychological reason to deny the incident or conflict and to avoid seeing the link between exacerbation of the anxiety disorder and the stressors. The key may be a symbolic reexperiencing or association with an initial trauma, which often is related to a disrupted relationship or present or past abuse.

(From Menninger, 1994, p. A88)

modality. Sometimes the treatment may begin with psychotherapy; sometimes, with pharmacotherapy. Ideally, these therapeutic modalities will operate synergistically, with psychotherapy enhancing the efficacy of the pharmacotherapy and vice versa. An integrated treatment approach acknowledges the reciprocal relationship between psychotherapy and pharmacotherapy and the interplay of transference and countertransference in the entire treatment process (Beitman, in press). Psychotherapists must acknowledge the significant efficacy of medications in alleviating the disabling symptoms of anxiety disorders. They must also appreciate the impact and meaning of medication at various stages of psychotherapy. Pharmacotherapists should appreciate the psychotherapeutic aspects of pharmacotherapy. The prescription of medication does not occur in a vacuum. It is inevitably part of a doctor-patient interaction. Thus, as pharmacotherapists prescribe and monitor medications, they are engaged in a psychotherapeutic interaction with patients. The way a pharmacotherapist handles the process can enhance or compromise the effects of the medication. The meaning of medication should be explored with the patient, both by the physician prescribing the medication and by the patient's psychotherapist (if there is a separate therapist).

In many respects, the challenges to providing integrated treatment are clear. Perhaps the final challenge is to disseminate more effectively the increasing knowledge of these disorders. We should be particularly cognizant of primary care physicians, those front-line practitioners who are increasingly called on to provide care and treatment for these patients.

References

Barlow, D.H. (1992). Cognitive-behavioral approaches to panic disorder and social phobia. *Bulletin of the Menninger Clinic, 56*(2, Suppl. A), A14-A28.

Beitman, B.D. (1995, March). *Integrating pharmacotherapy and psychotherapy.* Paper presented at the 17th annual Menninger Winter Psychiatry Conference, Park City, UT.

Beitman, B.D. (in press). Integrating pharmacotherapy and psychotherapy: An emerging field of study. *Bulletin of the Menninger Clinic.*

Borus, J.F., Howes, M.J., Devins, N.P., Rosenberg, R., & Livingston, W.W. (1988). Primary health care providers' recognition and diagnosis of mental disorders in their patients. *General Hospital Psychiatry, 10,* 317-321.

Chiles, J.A., Carlin, A.S., Benjamin, G.A.H., & Beitman, B.D. (1991). A physician, a nonmedical psychotherapist, and a patient: The pharmacotherapy-psychotherapy triangle. In B.D. Beitman & G.L. Klerman (Eds.), *Integrating pharmacotherapy and psychotherapy* (pp. 105-118). Washington, DC: American Psychiatric Press.

DuPont, R.L. (1995). Anxiety and addiction: A clinical perspective on comorbidity. In W.W. Menninger (Ed.), *Coping with anxiety: Integrated approaches to treatment* (pp. 51-69). Northvale, NJ: Aronson.

Eisenberg, L. (1992). Treating depression and anxiety in primary care: Closing the gap between knowledge and practice. *New England Journal of Medicine, 326,* 1080-1084.

Klerman, G.L. (1991). Ideological conflicts in integrating pharmacotherapy and psychotherapy. In B.D. Beitman & G.L. Klerman (Eds.), *Integrating pharmacotherapy and psychotherapy* (pp. 3-19). Washington, DC: American Psychiatric Press.

Marshall, J.R. (1995). Integrated treatment of social phobia. In W.W. Menninger (Ed.), *Coping with anxiety: Integrated approaches to treatment* (pp. 25-35). Northvale, NJ: Aronson.

Menninger, W.W. (1992). Integrated treatment of panic disorder and social phobia. *Bulletin of the Menninger Clinic, 56*(2, Suppl. A), A61-A70.

Menninger, W.W. (1994). Psychotherapy and integrated treatment of social phobia and comorbid conditions. *Bulletin of the Menninger Clinic, 58*(2, Suppl. A), A84-A90.

Ormel, J., Van den Brink, W., Koeter, M.W.J., Giel, R., Van der Meer, K., Van de Willige, G., & Wilmink, F.W. (1990). Recognition, management and outcome of psychological disorders in primary care: A naturalistic follow-up study. *Psychological Medicine, 20,* 909-923.

Regier, D.A., Narrow, W.E., & Rae, D.S. (1990). The epidemiology of anxiety disorders: The Epidemiologic Catchment Area (ECA) experience. *Journal of Psychiatric Research, 24*(2, Suppl.), 3-14.

Rosenbaum, J.F., & Pollock, R.A. (1994). The psychopharmacology of social phobia and comorbid disorders. *Bulletin of the Menninger Clinic, 58*(2, Suppl. A), A67-A83.

Rosenbaum, J.F., Pollock, R.A., Otto, M.W., & Pollack, M.H. (1995). Integrated treatment of panic disorder. In W.W. Menninger (Ed.), *Coping with anxiety: Integrated approaches to treatment* (pp. 1-23). Northvale, NJ: Aronson.

Shear, M.K., & Schulberg, H.C. (1995). Anxiety disorders in primary care. In W.W. Menninger (Ed.), *Coping with anxiety: Integrated approaches to treatment* (pp. 71-82). Northvale, NJ: Aronson.

Zerbe, K.J. (1995). Anxiety disorders in women. In W.W. Menninger (Ed.), *Coping with anxiety: Integrated approaches to treatment* (pp. 37-50). Northvale, NJ: Aronson.

Index